ADVANCE PRAISE

"Brian Murdoch is the rare combination of a leading medievalist and gifted translator. The volume is a joy to read, a brilliant and much-needed resource for teaching German poetry from its very beginnings. The selection from heroic epic via charms to religious songs also opens up new resources for conversation with those interested in Old English and other medieval literatures."
    – **Henrike Lähnemann**, *University of Oxford*

"*Old High German Poetry: An Anthology* opens up a treasure-hoard of extraordinary poems—from devotional verse, to heroic lyrics, to a metrical charm for capturing a hive of bees—to a wider audience. Each expertly edited poem is printed with a facing-page translation, offering the opportunity for instant comparison between the original and its English translation. These poetic gems sparkle under Brian Murdoch's touch as he applies his unparalleled erudition to every facet, which curious readers will treasure."
    – **Daniel Donoghue**, *Harvard University*

"This excellent edition makes the main body of Old High German poetry widely accessible to an English-speaking readership for the first time. Concise, engaging introductions contextualize the material effectively, while sensitive translations preserve as much as possible of the original verse form. The many linguistic, stylistic and topical parallels with other early Germanic literature make the volume a valuable source of comparative evidence for the study of Old English poetry."
    – **Carole Hough**, *University of Glasgow*

"With this comprehensive anthology of texts and translations, Brian Murdoch has done a great service for students and teachers of all medieval Germanic languages."

> **– Rolf H. Bremmer, Jr.,** *Leiden University*

"Every student of Old Norse benefits from becoming familiar with the fascinating works of Old High German poetry. Brian Murdoch has made this easier and more pleasant than ever before."

> **– Haukur Þorgeirsson,** *University of Iceland*

"The value of an anthology such as this cannot be underestimated. In contrast to Middle High German literature, particularly that of the twelfth and early thirteenth centuries, the corpus of works written in Old High German is relatively modest, but certainly not without significance from both a literary and linguistic standpoint. Professor Murdoch's anthology constitutes the only modern, bilingual Old High German to English edition available that contains all the major Old High German texts in a format that is eminently suited for both the student and the established scholar unfamiliar with the older German dialect. Furthermore, it offers an excellent overview of the German literary world between the ninth and eleventh century, from the heroic, and (possibly) fragmentary, ninth-century *Hildebrandslied*, through texts with a predominantly religious hue, to the late tenth-century historical narrative poem, *De Heinrico*. Apart from his translation of the Old High German texts, Professor Murdoch also offers for each a succinct, but lucid, commentary that situates the work within its literary and historical context as well as a selected bibliography of the most pertinent research.

This anthology by one of our profession's finest scholars will remind many former students of older German literature of a time when university departments of German offered courses in the literature and language not only of Middle High German, but also of Gothic, Old Saxon, Old Norse, and, of course, Old High German. This handsome volume will be welcomed not only by those specializing in these older Germanic dialects, but also by the non-German-speaking colleague who wishes to obtain a greater understanding of the literary culture of Germany between the ninth and the eleventh century. In this respect, Professor Murdoch is to be commended for having made an invaluable contribution to ensuring continuity within the fascinating field of Germanic Philology."

> **– Winder McConnell,** *University of California, Davis*

OLD HIGH GERMAN POETRY

AN ANTHOLOGY

Old High German Poetry

An Anthology

Edited and translated by

Brian Murdoch

UPPSALA BOOKS

London

To Hans Boehm

UPPSALA BOOKS

London, England

www.uppsalabooks.com

ISBN 978-1-961361-26-3 Hardback

ISBN 978-1-961361-27-0 Paperback

CONTENTS

INTRODUCTION

Old High German Poetry

The beginnings of German written literature (oral literature is a different tradition) lie in the late eighth century, and what is written over the next couple of centuries is in the language known as Old High German. This is itself not a unified language but is made up of a range of different dialects, all of which exhibit to some extent the effect of the so-called High German sound shift, which separated these dialects—broadly speaking from Aachen southwards—from Low German, which included Old Saxon and Old English. This stage of the language continues until around the middle of the eleventh century, when further changes move it into Middle High German. Two significant points need to be made about Old High German literature: first, there is not very much of it, and most of that is prose (a Gospel harmony, theological texts, a lot of glosses—individual words over their Latin equivalents); and secondly, it arises and remains firmly within the context of the Latin church. To these major considerations we have to add that—with one major exception—most of the poetry we have has survived more or less fortuitously, added into or even scrawled upon Latin theological or historical manuscripts, which have themselves occasionally been lost or stolen. Nearly all the texts as such have had to be restored to a certain extent.

Poetically, there is a major division between alliterative and end-rhymed verse. The earliest pieces are in the Germanic long line, with a caesura and the two parts linked by alliteration. There are far more examples of this elsewhere—in Old English and in Old Norse. Those examples that survive in Old High German are metrically often ragged in comparison. The alternative form, which establishes itself fairly soon and very thoroughly, and is associated in particular with Otfrid of Weissenburg, is of a similar long line, with each two-beat half-line rhymed at the end. These long lines are regularly set in strophes, usually of two such lines. The origin of this was probably in imitation of Latin hymns. There are occasional rhymed lines even in the alliterative poems.

Written Old High German depends in every respect upon the Latin church, which provided the skills, the impetus, and the wherewithal to write things down, however problematic the writing of a Germanic language might have been to those used to writing Latin. Dividing lines are, however, never absolute, and there has always been a justifiable interest in what has been preserved of pre-Christian cultures. Even though the Old High German texts were written down within a Christian context, one of the great works is the essentially Germanic heroic poem, the *Hildebrandslied*. Even in this poem the heroic central figure once invokes God, although an earlier version might very well have had a different invocation, and the passage is an awkward one metrically. Some of the charms, too, contain clear references to Germanic deities, and this is significant in its own right. It is of additional interest that a charm which refers to Wodan and other deities has survived hedged around (or perhaps simply 'accompanied') by Christian prayers. How well these pre-Christian names, some of which are not entirely clear, were known by the time they were written down, is matter of speculation, though some were doubtless familiar.

The most important figure in Old High German literature in the long term, however, is the monk, schoolmaster, and librarian Otfrid of Weissenburg, who lived through much of the ninth century. It is hard to stress his importance in this context enough. He is the first named poet, and the first who made (and explained) the conscious decision to write poetry, notably rhymed poetry, in German (he called it Frankish—his dialect was South Rhenish Franconian). He did so at length in a poetic presentation of the Gospels which survives not by the accidental chance that has given us most of the other pieces, but in a dedicated, well thought out, and beautifully produced manuscript in which his own script can be discerned. It was also copied at least three times. It was in effect an official publication. The work is in the rhymed form which would become standard, and the work has Latin headings and marginals. The substance, too, is not just the Gospels, but the Gospels as interpreted by medieval Latin exegesis. But it is still the first major written work in German that we have.

While even some very small fragments have been included here if they can be classified as poetry, it is perhaps worth noting here what is *not* included in the present anthology. Low German texts are omitted (although the major Old Saxon Gospel-poem known as *Heliand* is mentioned in passing in comparison with Otfrid's work). More importantly, no Latin texts are included, but this requires some elucidation. In a manuscript collection of Latin poems of German origin now in Cambridge (and containing what are referred to as the *Cambridge Songs*) are two macaronic texts— a form that mixes German and Latin—of which only one, *De Heinrico*, is included here; the other mixed text (*Suavissima nonna*) from that collection is too fragmentary to make much sense of. I have not included anything of *Ruodlieb*, a lengthy Latin verse adaptation of a folktale, which has four, but only four, Old High German words. As the Germanic-looking name of that work indicates, there may have been a German original, and the *Cambridge Songs* include several Latin pieces probably of German origin, some of which are occasionally found in anthologies of Old High German. There are several other longer Latin poems on themes that seem to be German, one important example of which is *Waltharius*, the Latin heroic epic of Walther of Aquitaine, for which we have Old English and other parallels. It may be based on a German (oral?) original. In some cases, too, we even know that there was indeed a German predecessor to a surviving Latin work. A monk from St Gallen called Ratpert wrote a poetic *Life of St Gall* which was translated into Latin, but that version is the only one we now have. There are several small pieces in Latin which may very plausibly be reckoned to have had German verse originals, and one, in fact, appears in what is actually recreated Old High German in the anthology by Karl Müllenhoff and Wilhelm Scherer (here referred to as MSD; see below *Texts and Abbreviations*), with the fact concealed in the notes that it actually survives only in Latin (MSD VIII). There is also a lullaby the authenticity of which is disputed. As indicated, many texts were glossed in Old High German, with interlinear German words added to the Latin texts, and some of these—where every word has been glossed— have been printed separately without the Latin original and look like poems, even though they are not: the German glosses to the *Murbach Hymns* and the *Carmen ad Deum,* for example, do not constitute poems in their own right. In chronological terms, finally, the line is drawn before texts like *Ezzos Gesang* or *Memento Mori,* the language of which begins to demonstrate features of Middle High German. A (very) few texts which do have poetic elements—a couple of charms—are omitted simply on the grounds that they are very confused.

I have translated some of the Latin material elsewhere: *Waltharius: The Latin Epic of Walther of Aquitaine* (ed. Leonard Neidorf, Uppsala Books, 2024), and two Cambridge Songs: *Heriger* (a humorous piece about an archbishop of Mainz, MSD XXV) in "Two Medieval Jollities," in *Peter Johnson: Feste Freundschrift* (ed. Hugh Ridley, Dublin: Conference of University Teachers of German, 1997), pp. 49–52; and *Modus Liebinc* (a comic anecdote about a snow-baby, MSD XXI) in my *The Grin of the Gargoyle* (Sawbridge: Dedalus, 1995), pp. 156–9.

The Translations

The translations offered are intended to keep as close to the originals as possible in line for line renderings, while conveying at the same time some indication at least of the poetic form. This is, of course, an entirely hubristic aim, and it is either a help (by permitting a certain freedom of approach) or an additional hindrance that, as noted, many of the texts survive in a somewhat parlous state. Aside from decipherment and linguistic difficulties, the few alliterative pieces we have do not compare well with examples in Old English or Old Norse. If the translations contain apparently 'incorrect' alliterative long lines, this is often true too of the poems. Rhymed verse is equally problematic. The translator is ever-conscious of the dangers of doggerel, and half-rhymes or near-rhymes are sometimes the only way out. However, the great innovator, Otfrid, also has rhymes which are by no means pure in modern terms, so that the translator is (almost) justified in hiding behind near-rhymes and assonances as well. There is, mercifully, only one macaronic poem in a fit state to be included. In principle, Latin passages are in italics in the translations.

Texts and Abbreviations

The texts are for the most part based on those in Elias von Steinmeyer, *Die kleineren althochdeutschen Sprachdenkmäler* (Berlin: Weidmann, 1916, repr. 1963), with occasional editing and capitalisation. I have given the text numbers not only from this collection, abbreviated as 'Steinmeyer,' but also from two further major text-sources: Karl Müllenhoff and Wilhelm Scherer, *Denkmäler deutscher Poesie und Prosa aus dem VIII–XII Jahrhundert*, 5th ed. by Elias von Steinmeyer (Berlin: Weidmann, 1892), abbreviated as 'MSD'; and from Wilhelm Braune, *Althochdeutsches Lesebuch*, cont. by Karl Helm, 17th ed. by Ernst Ebbinghaus (Tübingen: Niemeyer, 1994), abbreviated as 'Braune.' Editions of Otfrid's *Evangelienbuch* are listed separately in the relevant chapter (and in Otfrid the strophe-initials are capitalised in the manuscript and are here retained as such). A short introduction is provided for each text, with a few bibliographical references. A bibliography at the end of the work is in two parts: collections of the primary texts (some with modern German translations); and a list of what are, it is to be hoped, the most useful surveys of Old High German literature. In selecting secondary material, the emphasis is as far as possible on literary rather than purely linguistic studies, with some in English included where appropriate.

Acknowledgements

In looking through the bibliographies I am aware of how many scholars in this field I have known and learnt from (some sadly no longer with us), including a teacher, an examiner, a pupil, a co-author, and many colleagues: Linda Archibald, Cyril Edwards, John Flood, Dennis Green, Sidney Groseclose, Ruth Harvey, David McLintock, Ute Schwab, Hilda Swinburne, David Yeandle, and others. An enormous debt of gratitude, too, is due in the preparation of this anthology to Professor Leonard Neidorf, who first suggested the project and who has with his customary enthusiasm and expertise provided much assistance. I am also indebted to Wenbo Yang for his painstaking and enormously helpful scrutiny of the whole text. I am also grateful, as ever, for the support of my family.

Brian Murdoch   Stirling, 2025

1

The Lay of Hildebrand (*Hildebrandslied*)

The lay of Hildebrand is a mass of conflicts. It is the only early Germanic heroic poem preserved in German, although in what kind of German it is preserved (or was originally composed) is questionable. Although clearly in the Germanic alliterative verse-form, there are broken lines, some do not alliterate properly, some not at all. It seems to have been lightly Christianised. It survives in a somewhat ragged form, written down in the first half of the ninth century on the spare outside leaves of a biblical-theological manuscript (now in Kassel), one of which went missing after the Second World War and re-emerged in America years later (see W. F. Twaddell, "The *Hildebrandlied* Manuscript in the U.S.A. 1945– 1972". *Journal of English and Germanic Philology*. 73, 1974, 157– 168). We do not have an ending, though probably not much is missing and it is clear, on the basis of both internal and external evidence, that the father has to kill his son. Some of it has been copied badly, and it is possible that there are misplaced lines. In spite of all this, the poem is still a masterpiece.

The language seems to be a mixture of High and Low German, and it is assumed that someone tried to translate a poem probably composed in the eighth century in the Bavarian dialect of Old High German, into Low German (a few Anglo-Saxon letters are used, like the wynn-rune for w and sometimes a barred d), though some of the Low German forms are wrong or garbled. Some of the names suggest that an earlier version might have been Lombardic, the High German dialect from Northern Italy, and the context of the work takes us back to the Goths and the Huns in the fifth century. Attempts have been made to reconstruct the poem in Lombardic (which is very sparsely recorded) and indeed in Gothic. Reconstructions also remove the Christian elements in the poem, which can seem rather like *ad hoc* additions: one can imagine that line 49 once alliterated on *Wodan* rather than on *waltant got*, "ruling God."

The background implied in the work is the entirely unhistorical idea that Theoderic (Dietrich) the Ostrogoth, who made himself king of Rome, had originally been driven out of his kingdom by Odoaker (whom he killed, in fact). Theoderic is then placed anachronistically as an ally of Attila, king of the Huns (who died before the real Theoderic was born). Theoderic is supposed to have returned to reclaim his kingdom in a battle which seems to be the context of this poem. The poem itself depicts a fight between a father and his son (a theme occurring regularly in literature), something we are told in a single word almost immediately by a narrator whose comments are limited, but always significant. The rest is spoken (or perhaps thought) by the protagonists. Hildebrand and Hadubrand are the select champions from their respective armies—presumably those of Theoderic and of Odoaker respectively—and the names indicate that the warriors are related. The two armies play no further active part, but they—and the reader/listener—are the observing audience. To establish that each has a worthy opponent, the warriors say who they are. Hildebrand speaks first as the older man. His age is unusual, as we shall see, and later he declares that he has been undefeated in battle for thirty years. Now, however, he has to fight his son, and the winner will take the (valuable) armour of the defeated man. When asking the name of the opponent whom he ironically calls *chind* "child, young man," Hildebrand declares (ironically) that he knows all warrior families, but he hears that this man's father was called

Hildebrand. The son goes on to say that old wise men, who are (significantly) now dead have told him how Hildebrand fled with Theoderic, leaving behind in unhappy conditions a young bride and a very young or possibly even unborn child, "with no inheritance." The irony of it all is already clear: Hildebrand's rich armour is the son's missing inheritance, although what he clearly *has* inherited is prowess as a warrior. The son, resentful, but still proud of his father's reputation, cannot believe that a warrior as bold as his father can still be alive.

Now aware of the situation—as Hadubrand never is—Hildebrand declares that their relationship is the closest of all, but makes the mistake of offering as a gift a twisted golden arm-ring, which is, as the narrator now tells us, associated with the Huns. What it does is confirm for the younger man that his opponent actually *is* a Hun, and he refers to his father insultingly as such. Hadubrand also asserts unequivocally that he has been told by seafarers (further untraceable witnesses) that his father is dead. The tragedy is now inevitable—cruel fate will take its course. The only way that Hildebrand, who now thinks that he might as well *be* a Hun, can prove that he is indeed the great warrior he says he is, is to kill his own son, and the only way the son can obtain his inheritance is to earn it by killing his father.

The battle starts and is making rapid progress when the poem breaks off. Although the ending is missing, it is clear from parallel sources that the father kills the son: Hildibrandr kills Alibrandr in the Old Norse *Þiðrekssaga,* and he refers to killing his son in the *Ásmundarsaga kappabana.* A much later work called the *Jüngeres Hildebrandslied* has the two warriors return alive after the battle to the still-living wife, but this is hardly a likely outcome here. Hildebrand has to kill his son (and thus his entire line) if his warrior status is to be maintained. The only one who can understand the situation is Hildebrand himself, and even if Hadubrand had been victorious, the story would never have been known, and historically Hildebrand has to win for Theoderic. Even to fight to lose would negate his identity, and the only way in which he can confirm that identity is by the essentially unnatural act of killing his son, and thus his own posterity.

The text is principally that of Steinmeyer I, with some emendations—the text varies slightly in other editions: MSD II, Braune XXVIII. In the poem it is not always clear who is speaking or thinking, and it has also been argued (reasonably) that some of the dialogue should be shifted, although here the order is kept as in the manuscript. Lines 46–8 could fit into the final speech of the son and have been suggested as coming after lines 43. Although I adopted this change in an earlier translation in the Scottish *Lines Review* 109 (June 1989), pp. 20–22, it does not seem justified to do so here. Suggestions have also been made for emending lines (like 15 or 46) which do not seem to alliterate, but again I have kept to the received text.

There is predictably an enormous amount of secondary material concerned with this text, including several oddities, not just the Lombardic reconstruction, but also a psychological study, and even a work dedicated to showing that the poem is a forgery.

Elliott, Ralph W. V. "Byrhtnoth and Hildebrand: A Study in Heroic Technique." *Comparative Literature* 14 (1962): 53–70.

Gutenbrunner, Siegfried. *Von Hildebrand und Hadubrand: Lied-Sage-Mythos*. Heidelberg: Winter, 1976.

Lühr, Rosemarie. *Studien zur Sprache des Hildebrandsliedes*. Frankfurt am Main, Berne: Peter Lang, 1982.

McDonald, William C. "'Too Softly a Gift of Treasure': A Re-reading of the Old High German *Hildebrandslied*." *Euphorion* 78 (1984): 1–16.

Murdoch, Brian. *The Germanic Hero: Politics and Pragmatism in Early Medieval Poetry*. London: Hambledon, 1996, 34–46.

Norman, Frederick. *Three Essays on the Hildebrandslied*. London: Institute of Germanic Studies, 1973.

Renoir, Alain. "The Armor of the *Hildebrandslied*. An Oral-Formulaic Point of View." *Neuphilologische Mitteilungen* 78 (1977): 389–95.

Schwab, Ute and Maria Vittoria Molinari. *Ildebrando: Quattro saggi e i testi*. Alessandria: Edizioni dell'Orso, 2001. (essays in English, Italian and German, including one of those by Norman, above).

Hildebrandslied

Ik gihorta đat seggen,
đat sih urhettun   ænon muotin,
Hiltibrant enti Hađubrant   untar heriun tuem,
sunufatarungo.   Iro saro rihtun,
garutun se iro guđhamun,   gurtun sih iro suert ana,   5
helidos, ubar hringa,   do sie to dero hiltiu ritun.
Hiltibrant gimahalta [Heribrantes sunu]   — her uuas heroro man,
ferahes frotoro —;   her fragen gistuont
fohem uuortum,   wer sin fater wari
fireo in folche,   10
                         "eddo welihhes cnuosles du sis.
Ibu du mi enan sages,   ik mi de odre uuet,
chind, in chunincriche: chud ist mir al irmindeot."
Hadubrant gimahalta,   Hiltibrantes sunu
"dat sagetun mi   usere liuti,   15
alte anti frote,   dea erhina warun,
dat Hiltibrant haetti min fater;   ih heittu Hadubrant.
Forn her ostar giweit   — floh her Otachres nid —
hina miti Theotrihhe   enti sinero degano filu.
Her furlaet in lante   luttila sitten   20
prut in bure,   barn unwahsan
arbeo laosa.   He raet ostar hina,
des sid Detrihhe   darba gistuontun
fateres mines.   Dat uuas so friuntlaos man.
Her was Otachre   ummet tirri,   25
degano dechisto   miti Deotrichhe.
Her was eo folches at ente,   imo was eo fehta ti leop:
chud was her chonnem mannum.

The Lay of Hildebrand

I heard the tale told
how two fighters   came forward for combat,
Hildebrand and Hadubrand,   between two hosts,
a father and a son.   They set their weapons,
put on their battle gear,   girded on their swords
over chainmail,   as the champions rode out to fight.
Hildebrand, son of Heribrand, spoke,   having the right of age,
a well-tried warrior,   he wanted to find out
in a few words,   the father of his enemy,
his family and clan.
                         "Or who your kinsmen are.
If you name me one,   I shall know the others.
I know well   every warrior family in the land."
Hadubrand spoke,   Hildebrand's son:
"I have been told   by our people,
old and learned men   who lived long ago,
that my father's name was Hildebrand.   Hadubrand is mine.
He fled into eastern exile   from Odoaker's anger,
far away with Theoderic   and many of his thanes,
and at home he left,   lost and bereft,
a young bride   and a baby barely born,
with no inheritance,   as eastwards he fled.
Since then Theoderic   must have thought it hard
to lose my father,   friendless exile as he was.
He bore towards Odoaker   only hatred,
as the truest of the thanes   with Theoderic.
Always first in the field,   fighting was his delight.
He was well-known   to all warriors.

Ni waniu ih iu lib habbe."
"wettu irmingot [quad Hiltibrant]   obana ab heuane,   30
dat du neo dana halt mit sus sippan man
dinc ni gileitos."
Want her do ar arme   wuntane bauga,
cheisuringu gitan,   so imo se der chuning gap,
Huneo truhtin: "dat ih dir it nu bi huldi gibu."   35
Hadubrant gimalta,   Hiltibrantes sunu
"mit geru scal man   geba infahan,
ort widar orte.
Du bist dir alter Hun,   ummet spaher,
spenis mih mit dinem wortun,   wili mih dinu speru werpan, 40
pist also gialtet man,   so du ewin inwit fuortos.
Dat sagetun mi   seolidante
westar ubar wentilseo,   dat inan wie furnam.
Tot ist Hiltibrant,   Heribrantes suno."
Hiltibrant gimahalta,   Heribrantes suno   45
"Wela gisihu ih in dinem hrustim,
dat du habes heme   herron goten,
dat du noh bi desemwo riche   reccheo niwurti.
Welaga nu, waltant got,"   [quad Hiltibrant] "wewurt skihit.
Ih wallota sumaro enti wintro   sehstic ur lante,   50
dar man mih eo scerita   in folc sceotantero:
so man mir at burc enigeru   banun ni gifasta,
nu scal mih suasat chind   suertu hauwan,
breton mit sinu billiu,   eddo ih imo ti banin werdan.
Doh maht du nu aodlihho,   ibu dir din ellen taoc,   55
in sus heremo man   hrusti giwinnan,
rauba birahanen,   ibu du dar enic reht habes.
Der si doh nu argosto [quad Hiltibrant]   ostarliuto,
der dir nu wiges warne,   nu dih es so wel lustit,
gudea gimeinun: niuse de motti,   60
werdar sih hiutu   dero hregilo rumen muotti
erdo desero brunnono   bedero uualtan."

I am sure he is dead now."
"By God," said Hildebrand,   "by heaven's ruler,
before now, no man so close in blood
has been your adversary..."
He took from his arm   a twisted torque
of imperial gold,   given him by a king,
the Hun's overlord.   "Have this for friendship."
Hadubrand spoke,   Hildebrand's son:
"Tokens like that   should be taken at spear's length,
sharp point against sharp point!
Old Hun,   you are all trickery,
spinning webs of words,   wanting to spear me through.
You have only lived so long   by lies and deceit.
It was said to me   by seamen
who fared on the western ocean   that he fell in battle.
Hildebrand is dead,   Heribrand's son."
Hildebrand spoke,   Heribrand's son:
"I can see well from your battle-gear
that your commander   cares well for his men
and you have never had   the hardship of exile.
God's curse on it," said Hildebrand,   "cruel fate takes its course.
I have spent sixty winters   and summers as a wanderer,
ever in the forefront   of the fiercest fighting
and was never felled   before any fortress,
but now my own son's   sword will cut me down,
bring me low,   or I shall be his bane.
It should not be hard,   if you have the strength,
to take from such an old man   his arms and battle-gear,
and keep the rich spoils   if you have any right to them.
Hildebrand said: "Only the most craven wretch of the eastern race
would waver,   since you so much want to fight,
so let us try   in the test of strength
to see which fighter   must forfeit his weapons,
or who will carry off   both coats of mail."

Do lettun se ærist   asckim scritan,
scarpen scurim: dat in dem sciltim stont.
Do stoptun to samane   staimbortchludun,   65
heuwun harmlicco   huitte scilti,
unti im iro lintun   luttilo wurtun,
giwigan miti wabnum...

First in the fight   flew ash-wood spears,
sharp and strong;   they struck into the shields,
the men closed in   clashing ironclad bucklers,
hacked wildly   at the whitewood boards,
till the linden split   and splintered
broken by the blades...

2

The Wessobrunn Creation and Prayer (*Wessobrunner Gebet*)

The brief creation-poem and prayer from an otherwise Latin manuscript (now in Munich) from the monastery of Wessobrunn in Bavaria (it may have originated elsewhere) is neatly and clearly written, with the Latin heading *De poeta*, which seems to mean "on the creator." The capitals in the manuscript, which has been much reproduced, are followed here, and the prefix *ga-* in some of the words is represented with an unusual "star" rune. The word *enti*, "and," is represented by a standard abbreviation, and there is clearly something missing in line 4 (*ni nohheinig*, "nor any...")—a reference to the stars was assumed at an early stage and is probably correct. The layout of the text has been discussed, and lines 10–16 are sometimes put as prose, but other critics (notably Ute Schwab and Cyril Edwards) take the whole as an alliterative poem, and that is followed here. It was probably composed at the end of the eighth or the early ninth century, perhaps linked with the Anglo-Saxon mission to Germany, and is, with the *Hildebrand* poem, one of the early alliterative pieces in Old High German, although there is evidence of rhyme as well. Its dialect is Bavarian. The work falls into two parts: the first is a presentation of the void before the creation of the world, when only God existed; the second part, following on from a formulaic reference to "almighty

God," is a straightforward prayer for the grace of faith and the wisdom and strength to resist the devil. The text is Steinmeyer II, MSD I, and Braune XXIX.

Edwards, Cyril and Jennie Kiff-Hooper. "Ego bonefacius scripsi? More Oblique Approaches to the Wessobrunn Prayer." In *Mit regulu bithuungan: Neue Arbeiten zur althochdeutschen Poesie und Sprache,* edited by John L. Flood and David N. Yeandle, 94–122. Göppingen: Kümmerle, 1989.

Schwab, Ute. "Zum 'Wessobrunner Gebet': Eine Vorstellung und neue Lesungen" [1988/9]. In *Weniger wäre: Ausgewählte kleine Schriften,* edited by Astrid van Nahl and Onga Middel, 349–384. Vienna: Fassbaender, 2003.

Seiffert, Leslie. "The Metrical Form and Composition of the *Wessobrunner Gebet." Medium Aevum* 31 (1962): 1–13.

Wessobrunner Gebet

De poeta

Dat gafregin ih mit firahim   firiuuizzo meista,
dat ero niuuas   noh ufhimil,
noh paum...   noh pereg niuuas,
ni ... nohheinig   noh sunna niscein,
noh mano niliuhta   noh der mareo seo.   5
Do dar niuuiht niuuas   enteo ni uuenteo,
enti do uuas der eino   almahtico cot,
manno miltisto,   enti dar uuarun auh manake mit inan
cootlihhe geista,   enti cot heilac.

Cot almahtico,   du himil enti erda gauuorahtos   10
enti du mannun   so manac coot forgapi,
forgip mir in dino ganada   rehta galaupa
enti cotan uuilleon,   uuistom enti spahida enti craft
tiuflun za uuidarstantanne   enti arc za piuuisanne
enti dinan uuilleon   za gauurchanne.   15

The Wessobrunn Creation and Prayer

Of the Creator

I learned from wise men,   the most wondrous marvel,
that there was no earth   nor any sky above,
no trees grew,   there were no great mountains,
no [stars] were seen   nor the sun's shining
nor did the moon light up   the mighty sea.
When there was nothing,   no end and no beginning,
there was alone   almighty God,
most wondrous of beings,   and with him were
many good spirits,   and God [is] the most holy.

Almighty God,   who made heaven and earth,
and who to mankind gave   so much goodness,
by your grace bestow on me   belief that is true,
good will,   wisdom, wit, and strength
to resist all devils   and to avoid evil,
and to work   your will.

3

The Last Judgement (*Muspilli*)

The poem known as *Muspilli* again survives by chance only. The text is written on the blank pages, margins, and even (*horribile dictu*) on the dedication page of a fine Latin manuscript that had been presented to King Ludwig the German (Ludwig II, King of the East Franks), who died in 876. The chaotic transmission makes it difficult to establish an entirely coherent version, and it is in any case a fragment, albeit of just over a hundred lines. Its dialect is Bavarian, and it seems to have been written down in the second half of the ninth century, composed slightly earlier, and perhaps revised. It is grouped with the *Hildebrandslied* and the Wessobrunn poem in that it is composed in the traditional Germanic alliterative verse-form, although once more some of its lines are imperfect, or are rhymed.

The name of the piece is itself a problem. The first editor in the nineteenth century took as the title a word from the text which, however memorable, is a *hapax legomenon* in Old High German. It appears to mean—from comparing it with other Germanic sources—something like "the destruction of the world by fire." What title, then, can a translator give it? The eschaton? Apocalypse? Doomsday? The *dies irae* ("heaven and earth in ashes ending")? *Ragnarök*? The last days? The world's last night?

Judgement day? Since there is a legal element in the poem, at least retaining the idea of judgement seems appropriate.

The work is a poetic sermon with a sequence of different themes. It begins with the death of the individual and the battle for the soul of the departed, then moves to an apocalyptic picture of the end of the world and the last judgement, of which two versions are presented. In one, Elias (Elijah) fights with the Antichrist, and wins (a tradition found in some apocryphal texts), but in the other he is defeated, and his blood causes the final destruction of all things. That second version is based on the Bible, in Revelation (Apocalypse) 11, 3–12, where the "two witnesses" are traditionally interpreted as Enoch and Elias/Elijah. At the last judgement, we are then told, when a man comes before the judge, it is best that he judged well himself when on earth, and evildoing on earth will deliver him up to the devil. The final part of the work describes the last days, the horn will sound, and the dead will rise and be judged. Then the poem breaks off.

The work has been linked with the last part of an Anglo-Saxon text in the Exeter Book, *Christ* III, where there are some similarities, but apocalyptic visions are a very broad tradition. It has been suggested that this work was written as a sermon directed at an aristocratic audience, men who might well have sat in judgement over others, which may also have determined the decision to compose a piece in what was already becoming an old-fashioned heroic-alliterative style.

The text (Steinmeyer XIV, MSD III, Braune XXX) has necessarily been emended over the years, line-numbering varies and the (partly indecipherable) lines 74a and 99a remain questionable. Steinmeyer famously made a despairing comment in the notes in his edition, and here the text in Braune has also been followed. Much of the extensive secondary literature is concerned with the transmission, language, and structure of the poem. Cola Minis attempted a reconstruction of a proposed original.

Finger, Heinz. *Untersuchungen zum "Muspilli."* Göppingen: Kümmerle, 1977.

Hagen, Sivert N. "Muspilli." *Modern Philology* 1 (1904): 397–409.

Kolb, Herbert. "*Vora demo muspille.* Versuch einer Interpretation." *Zeitschrift für deutsches Altertum* 83 (1964): 2–33.

Manganella, Gemma. "*Muspilli.* Problemi i interpretazioni." *Annali dell'Istituto Orientale di Napoli/Sez.* Germ. 3 (1960): 17–49.

Minis, Cola. *Handschrift, Form und Sprache des Muspilli.* Berlin: Schmidt, 1966. (Reviewed by Leslie Seiffert. *Modern Language Review* 64 (1969): 206–208).

Mohr, Wolfgang and Walter Haug. *Zweimal "Muspilli."* Tübingen: Niemeyer, 1977. (Reviewed by Brian Murdoch. *Medium Aevum* 47 (1978): 340–342).

Pakis, Valentine A. "The Literary Status of *Muspilli* in the History of Scholarship." *Amsterdamer Beiträge zur älteren Germanistik* 65 (2009): 41–60.

Spechtler, Franz Viktor. "Altes und neues Recht. Bemerkungen über neue Forschungen zum althochdeutschen 'Muspilli'." *Amsterdamer Beiträge zur älteren Germanistik* 15 (1980): 39–52.

Venosa, Elena di. *Muspilli. Introduzione, Traduzione e Commento.* Pisa: Pisa University Press, 2023.

Muspilli

... sin tac piqueme,   daz er touuan scal,
uuanta sar so sih diu sela   in den sind arheuit
enti si den lihhamun   likkan lazzit,
so quimit ein heri   fona himilzungalon,
daz andar fona pehhe: dar pagant siu umpi.   5
Sorgen mac diu sela,   unzi diu suona arget,
za uuederemo herie   si gihalot uuerde,
uuanta ipu sia daz Satanazses   kisindi kiuuinnit,
daz leitit sia sar,   dar iru leid uuirdit,
in fuir enti in finstri: daz ist rehto uirinlih ding.   10
Upi sia auar kihalont die,   die dar fona himile quemant,
enti si dero engilo   eigan uuirdit,
die pringent sia   sar uf in himilo rihi:
dar ist lip ano tod,   lioht ano finstri,
selida ano sorgun: dar nist neoman siuh.   15
denne der man in pardisu   pu kiuuinnit,
hus in himile,   dar quimit imo hilfa kinuok.
Pidiu ist durft mihhil
allero manno uuelihemo,   daz in es sin muot kispane,
daz er kotes uuillun   kerno tuo   20
enti hella fuir   harto uuise,
pehhes pina: dar piutit der Satanasz altist
heizzan lauc.   So mac huckan za diu,
sorgen drato,   der sih suntigen uueiz.
Uue demo in uinstri scal   sino uirina stuen,   25
prinnan in pehhe: daz ist rehto paluuic dink,
daz der man haret ze gote   enti imo hilfa niquimit.
Uuanit sih kinada   diu uuenaga sela:

The Last Judgement

... his day comes,   when die he must,
when his soul   sets off on its path,
and the corpse, lifeless,   is left lying.
Then comes a host   of heavenly beings
and also a force from hell   to fight for that soul.
The soul will be in dread   until the doom is declared,
of which of the two   is to take it away,
for if Satan's men   manage to win,
they will carry the soul   where suffering awaits,
with darkness and fire.   That is a fearsome fate!
But if the soul is held   by the heavenly hosts,
and belongs alone   to all the angels,
they will carry it up   to the kingdom of heaven.
There is life without death   light without darkness,
a home without hardship,   and with health everlasting.
For if a man wins a place   in Paradise,
a home in heaven,   all help shall be his.
Therefore there is great need
that all men must   be mindful and should
carry out gladly   God's will,
and ever flee   from the fires of hell,
the burning pitch   prepared by old Satan
with hot flames,   and fear the thought,
if he is certain   that he has sinned.
Woe to the man doomed   to the dark dungeon,
to burn in those fires,   a most fearsome fate –
he howls to God   and help does not come.
The wretched soul   still seeks grace,

niist in kihuctin   himiliskin gote,
uuanta hiar in uuerolti   after niuuerkota.   30
so denne der mahtigo khuninc   daz mahal kipannit,
dara scal queman   chunno kilihaz.
Denne nikitar parno nohhein   den pan furisizzan,
ni allero manno uuelih   ze demo mahale sculi.
Dar scal er uora demo rihhe   az rahhu stantan,   35
pi daz er in uuerolti   kiuuerkot hapeta.
Daz hortih rahhon   dia uueroltrehtuuison,
daz sculi der antichristo   mit Eliase pagan.
Der uuarch ist kiuuafanit: denne uuirdit untar in uuic arhapan.
Khenfun sint so kreftic,   diu kosa ist so mihhil.   40
Elias stritit   pi den euuigon lip,
uuili den rehtkernon   daz rihhi kistarkan:
pidiu scal imo helfan   der himiles kiuualtit.
Der antichristo   stet pi demo altfiante,
stet pi demo Satanase,   der inan uarsenkan scal: 45
pidiu scal er in deru uuicsteti   uunt piuallan
enti in demo sinde   sigalos uuerdan.
Doh uuanit des uilo   gotmanno,
daz Elias in demo uuige   aruuartit uuerde.
So daz Eliases pluot   in erda kitriufit,   50
so inprinnant die perga,   poum nikistentit
enihc in erdu,   aha artruknent,
muor uarsuuilhit sih,   suilizot lougiu der himil,
mano uallit,   prinnit mittilagart,
sten nikistentit.   Uerit denne stuatago in lant,   55
uerit mit diu uuiru   uiriho uuison.
Dar nimac denne mak andremo   helfan uora demo muspille.
Denne daz preita uuasal   allaz uarprinnit
enti uuir enti luft   iz allaz arfurpit,
uuar ist denne diu marha, dar man dar eo mit sinen magon piehc? 60
Diu marha ist farprunnan,   diu sela stet pidungan,
niuueiz mit uuiu puaze: so uerit si za uuize.

but is now no more   in the mind of God
since here in the world   his works were not worthy.
When the King of Glory   calls for judgement,
then all men's kin   must come there,
and no child shall dare   deny the doom,
or think any man   might miss the judgement.
Before the great judge   he must give account
Of all his works   in the world of men.
Men who are wise   in the world's laws
have told me that Antichrist   and Elias will fight.
The beast is well-armed,   then their battle will begin,
such strong warriors,   for the worthiest cause.
Elias fights   for eternal life
and to reinforce   the realms of the righteous.
He shall be helped   by heaven's lord.
The Antichrist stands   with the old enemy,
on the side of Satan,   who will see him fall
on that battlefield   broken and wounded,
left lying,   having lost the war.
Yet it has been said   by many men of God
that Elias in that battle   will be beaten,
and when the blood of Elias   falls on the earth,
mountains shall burn,   all trees shall break
the whole earth shall see   the seas run dry,
the moors all swallowed up,   the skies aflame,
the moon shall fall   and middle-earth be burned,
no stone will stand   when doomsday stalks the land
with burning fires   to beset mankind.
No man can aid his kinsman   when he comes to Judgement Day,
when the entire earth   is all aflame,
and fire and wind   wipe all things away.
Where then are the bounds   bargained over by you and your kinsmen?
All boundaries are burned away,   and the soul stands in dismay,
unable to make amends   and is eternally damned.

Pidiu ist demo manne so guot,   denner ze demo mahale quimit,
daz er rahono   uueliha rehto arteile.
Denne nidarf er sorgen,   denne er ze deru suonu quimit.   65
niuueiz der uuenago man,   uuielihan uuartil er habet,
denner mit den miaton   marrit daz rehta,
daz der tiuual dar pi   kitarnit stentit.
Der hapet in ruouu   rahono uueliha,
daz der man er enti sid   upiles kifrumita,   70
daz er iz allaz kisaget,   denne er ze deru suonu quimit.
Niscolta sid manno nohhein   miatun intfahan.
So daz himilisca   horn kilutit uuirdit
enti sih der [suanari]   ana den sind arheuit,
[der dar suannan scal,   toti enti lepenten],   74a
denne heuit sih mit imo   herio meista,   75
daz ist allaz so pald,   daz imo nioman kipagan nimak.
Denne uerit er ze deru mahalsteti,   deru dar kimarchot ist:
dar uuirdit diu suona,   die man dar io sageta.
Denne uarant engila   uper dio marha,
uuechant deota,   uuissant ze dinge.   80
Denne scal manno gilih   fona deru moltu arsten,
lossan sih ar dero leuuo uazzon: scal imo auar sin lip piqueman,
daz er sin reht allaz   kirahhon muozzi
enti imo after sinen tatin   arteilit uuerde.
Denne der gisizzit,   der dar suonnan scal   85
enti arteillan scal   toten enti quekkhen,
denne stet dar umpi   engilo menigi,
guotero gomono: gart ist so mihhil;
dara quimit ze deru rihtungu so uilo,   dia dar ar resti arstent.
So dar manno nohhein   uuiht pimidan nimak,   90
dar scal denne hant sprehhan,   houpit sagen,
allero lido uuelihc   unzi in den luzigun uinger,
uuaz er untar desen mannun   mordes kifrumita.
Dar niist eo so listic man,   der dar iouuiht arliugan megi,
daz er kitarnan megi   tato dehheina,   95

When called to that court   it counts most for a man
if the judgements he gave   were also just,
for then he need have no cares   when he comes to the court.
The wretched soul never   knows who watches him,
or knows if he with payments   has perverted the law,
or that there is the devil,   who has many disguises,
who calmly details   every dark deed
of that man, done early   or done after,
so he can tell of it all   when he comes to the trial,
Far better then,   not to have been bribed.
When the heavenly   horn rings out,
and the judge comes   to that court
to pass judgement on the living and the dead,
He shall have with him   the greatest of heaven's hosts,
a force so strong   that none can strive against them.
He will come to the place   put aside for this,
where sentence will be passed   as has always been said.
Then the angels' band   will fly over the land,
waking all folk   to follow them to the court.
Then every dead man   from dust must rise up,
break the grave's bonds,   take his body back,
so that he can   account for himself,
and according to his deeds   hear his doom.
Then God shall take his seat   to pass sentence,
that judgement be dealt   on the quick and the dead,
and with Him will stand   the angelic band,
and so many of the holy   in that huge place,
to which crowds come to trial   taken from their tombs.
No man can ever   conceal a thing,
his hand will bear witness,   his head will speak,
and all his limbs   down to the littlest finger
will recount dreadful deeds   done to his fellow men.
No cheat can dare   to deny or to lie,
or attempt to hide   any of his acts.

niz al fora demo khuninge   kichundit uuerde,
uzzan er iz mit alamusanu furimegi
enti mit fastun   dio uirina kipuazti.
Denne der paldet,   der gipuazzit hapet.
[denner ze deru suonu quimit.]   99a
uuirdit denne furi kitragan   daz frono chruci,   100
dar der heligo Christ   ana arhangan uuard.
Denne augit er dio masun,   dio er in deru m[enniski anfenc],
dio er duruh desse mancunnes   minna [fardoleta...]

All things will be counted   by the mighty king,
unless the man has atoned   with almsgiving,
and has paid for his crimes   with the penance of fasting.
He may be at peace,   if he was penitent,
when he comes to the judgement seat.
Then shall be carried out   the sacred cross
on which there hung   Holy Christ.
He shall display the wounds   that he wore as a man,
suffered harm for the love   of humankind...

4

Charms

The Old High German texts referred to as charms are—because they were all recorded within a Christian context—principally collects, i.e., prayers asking for the amelioration of a particular (usually medical) condition affecting either humans or their most important animals (horses, dogs, bees). The actual prayers added to these charms are Latin, of course, but the charms also incorporate German passages, sometimes poetic, which tell a story linked with the situation to be remedied. Typically a charm would contain some or all of a set of different elements, some in Latin, others in the vernacular: an indication of the purpose; instructions for action; an utterance ("magic words"); a spoken narrative (*historiola*); a command that the patient be (similarly) healed; further instruction to repeat the charm or prayers (usually the Paternoster); an assurance that the charm will work. Charms are, of course, known from a great many cultures, and there are official church prayers—collects—for these situations too, and particular saints may be invoked for individual ailments. Most of the Old High German charms were presumably incantatory (a periapt is a written talisman), but the story parts are frequently in prose, even if they have a kind of poetic feel; thus the epilepsy charm *contra caducum morbum,* "on the falling sickness," has some parallel phrases, but is neither alliterative nor rhymed. It contains, incidentally, what is probably a reference to the god Donar, Thor, in an opening invocation which is hard to elucidate, although it goes on to refer to Satan and Adam. Some of these charms are very difficult to interpret and can appear positively garbled, as for example a haemostatic charm from a (now lost) Strasbourg manuscript, which is not included here because although it has rhymed parts, it is almost impossible to interpret. The same applies to the very difficult horse-charm *Contra rehin*, from a medical manuscript, and about which Steinmeyer once again seems to have despaired. The epilepsy charm mentioned above, which is known in two versions, has also defied proper interpretation and may or may not mention a Germanic god. What is offered here, therefore, is a selection only of those that are clearly High German (some have Low German parallels) and clearly poetic, either in alliterative long-lines, or with at least some rhymed passages. Precise dating is predictably difficult. The charms may appear added to Latin theological manuscripts, or are found in more coherent medical collections. A very few actual medical recipes have, incidentally, also been preserved in Old High German.

One obvious question is whether these charms worked, and the fact that they were written down at all means the answer is likely to have been affirmative, albeit in a qualified sense. The repeated concluding prayers may well have calmed the patient and given time for any other measures (like binding a wound or calming an epileptic seizure) to take effect. There are charms for a number of eventualities, from the relatively trivial (bleeding, nosebleeds, sore eyes, sore throats) to fevers, gout, and indeed epilepsy, or even unspecified diseases caused by "worms." All kinds of maladies for horses are catered for, though in our less horse-dependent society we are now not always certain what exactly they were. There is, of course, an overlap between charms and blessings; one of the latter, from Weingarten, is included in another section, but the rather different and more simply structured verses intended to repel devils or keep them out of the house are closer to charms.

Once again, although these charms all survive in a written Christian context, there are some clear references to Germanic gods, something which has always attracted great interest. In the second Merseburg charm, it is Wodan who works the spell. The appended prayers will have rendered the narrative portions respectable, intended to override the paganism. They command cures—provided it is the will of God. Some of the Germanic gods invoked are even now still familiar. Overall, most of the surviving Old High German charms are entirely Christian, although even if they do refer to biblical figures, the narratives often derive from apocryphal or pseudepigraphic, rather than canonical texts. The Jordan stands still in some of the blood-charms, and this is a tale found in various non-canonical works rather than in the Gospels.

The alliterative *Merseburger Zaubersprüche*, the East Franconian charms from a tenth-century manuscript in Merseburg clearly preserve earlier material, but it is not absolutely clear what they are for. The first (if they are indeed separate) has been claimed as a charm for releasing prisoners, and there are references to such charms elsewhere in Germanic literature: in the Norse *Hávamál*, Odin knows such a charm, for example. On the other hand, escape from something like the bonds of cramp might be equally possible. The second charm, after what looks like the letter H, which may mean *item* "another," refers to an incident with a horse, but might (also) be applicable for any cramp, strain or sprain, equine or human. Wodan is clear, but some of the other names are not, especially Phol. The Latin prayer (here truncated) remains an important part of the work. *Pro Nessia* (Bavarian) is found in a ninth-century Munich manuscript and there is a Low German version (*Contra vermes*). The first line is alliterative, but some of the others are not, and are in any case too word-specific to imitate in English. Presumably the arrow was then shot away to get rid of the disease-bringing worms, a ritual found in charms in other cultures. The *Bamberger Blutsegen,* which mixes (rhythmic) prose and clear rhyme, is an East Franconian haemostatic charm found in a late twelfth-century medical miscellany. The somewhat confused *Ad fluxum sanguinis narium* (a Low German version is clearer) is from another medical miscellany, now in Paris, with other German material including the horse charm *Ad equum errehet* (eleventh- or twelfth-century Rhenish-Franconian). The Rhenish Franconian *Lorscher Bienensegen* is ninth- or tenth-century (with a parallel in Old English), designed to stop the valuable honey-source from swarming elsewhere; the Latin theological manuscript from Lorsch, near Frankfurt, in which this charm was written, is now in the Vatican. The final three pieces are to combat devils and are thus on the borderline between charms and prayers. *Ad signandum domum contra diabolum* is from Zurich (tenth century, Alemannic), and the word the devil cannot say is baffling, but alliterative, although no guarantees can be offered on its efficacy. The Rhenish Franconian *Trierer Spruch wider den Teufel,* was written in a crude code in the eleventh century in a ninth-century theological manuscript, most of the vowels replaced by the following letter of the alphabet (as *cplbpn* for *colbon*). The final *Reimspruch*, which is also from Trier (a late tenth-century manuscript now in the British Library, more or less Rhenish Franconian) is a translation of a Latin sentence from Gregory the Great meaning "no-one should fear the devil because he can do nothing without permission."

The texts are based on Steinmeyer LXII-LXIX and LXXV-LXXXI (see Braune XXXI; they are somewhat scattered in MSD) with layout and punctuation adapted. There is again a large body of secondary work, not always entirely convincing.

Abernethy, George William. *The Germanic Metrical Charms*. University of Wisconsin: Doctoral Dissertation, 1983.

Cianci, Eleonora. *Incantesimi e benedizioni nella letteratura tedesca medievale (IX–XIII sec)*. Göppingen: Kümmerle, 2004.

Eis, Gerhard. *Altdeutsche Zaubersprüche*. Berlin: de Gruyter, 1964.

Fuller, Susan. "Pagan Charms in Tenth-Century Saxony? The Function of the Merseburg Charms." *Monatshefte* 72 (1980):

162–170 (with a "Rejoinder" by Heather Stuart and F. Walla in *Germanic Notes* 14 (1983): 35–37).

Hampp, Irmgard. "Vom Wesen des Zaubers im Zauberspruch." *Der Deutschunterricht* 13/1 (1961): 58–76.

Helm, Karl. "Zur althochdeutschen 'Hausbesegnung'." *Beiträge zur Geschichte der deutschen Sprache und Literatur* 69 (1947): 358–361.

Jongeboer, Henk. "Der Lorscher Bienensegen und der ags. Charm *wiþ ymbe*." *Amsterdamer Beiträge zur älteren Germanistik* 21 (1984): 63–70.

Miller, Carol Ann. *The Old High German and Old Saxon Charms.* Washington University: Doctoral Dissertation, 1963.

Murdoch, Brian. "But Did They Work? Interpreting the Old High German Merseburg Charms in their Medieval Context." *Neuphilologische Mitteilungen* 89 (1988): 358–369.

Murdoch, Brian. "*Drohtin, uuerthe so!* Zur Funktionsweise der althochdeutschen Zaubersprüche." *Jahrbuch der Görres-Gesellschaft* NS 32 (1991): 11–37.

Merseburger Zaubersprüche

Eiris sazun idisi,   sazun hera duoder.
Suma hapt heptidun,   suma heri lezidun,
suma clubodun   umbi cuoniouuidi.
Insprinc haptbandun,   inuar uigandun!
H
Phol ende uuodan   uuorun zi holza.
Du uuart demo balderes uolon   sin uuoz birenkit.
Thu biguolen sinthgunt,   sunna era suistor,
thu biguolen friia,   uolla era suister,
thu biguolen uuodan,   so he uuola conda:
sose benrenki,   sose bluotrenki,
sose lidirenki:
ben zi bena,   bluot zi bluoda,
lid zi geliden,   sose gelimida sin!

Om[ni]p[otens] s[ancte] pater n[oster] d[eus] qui facis mirabilia
magna solus, p[rae]tende super famulu[m] tuu[m] N... per [do-
minum nostrum Jesum Christum].

Pro Nessia
Gang uz, Nesso,   mit niun nessinchilinon,
uz fonna marge   in deo adra,
vonna den adrun   in daz fleisk,
fonna demu fleiske   in daz fel,
fonna demo velle   in diz tulli.
Ter Pater noster.

The Merseburg Charms

Once women were sitting,   sitting here and there.
Some fixed chains,   some fended off the forces,
some broke open   the bonds.
Escape from the fetters!   Flee the foe!
H
Phol and Wodan   in the woods rode,
where Balder's foal   its foot sprained.
Then Sinthgund spoke over it,   Sunna's sister
then Freya spoke over it,   Folla's sister,
then Wodan spoke over it,   as he was well able.
Be it bone-wrench,   be it blood-wrench
be it limb-wrench,
bone to bone,   blood to blood,
limb to limb,   locked together as if limed!

*Omnipotent holy father, our God, who alone performs great miracles,
look down upon your servant N... through Jesus Christ our lord.*

Against disease-worms
Begone, worm   with nine wee wormlets,
out of the marrow   into the veins
out of the veins   into the flesh
out of the flesh,   into the skin
out of the skin   into this arrow.
Three Paternosters.

Bamberger Blutsegen

Crist unte Iudas spiliten mit spieza. do wart der heiligo Xrist wnd in sine siton.

do namer den dvmen. unte uorduhta se uorna. So uerstant du bluod. sose Iordanis aha uerstunt. do der heiligo Iohannes den heilanden Crist in iro tovfta. daz dir zo bvza.
Crist wart hi[en] erden wunt.   Daz wart da ze himele chunt.
Iz neblvotete, noch nesvar.   Noch nechein eiter nebar.
Taz was ein file göte stunte.   Heil sis tu wnte!

In nomine Ih[esu Christi], daz dir ze bvze. Pat[er noster]. ter. Et addens hoc it[em] ter. Ich besuere dich bi den heiligen fu[n]f wnten. heil sis tu wnde. et P[er] patre[m].+ et filiu[m].+ et sp[iritum] s[anctu]m.+ fiat. fiat. amen.

Ad fluxum sanguinis narium
Christ unde Iohan   giengon zuo der Iordan.
Do sprach Christ:"stant, Iordan,   biz ih unde lohan uber dih gegan".
Also Iordan do stuont,   so stant du .N. illivs bluot.
Hoc dicat[ur] ter et singulis uicib[us] fiat nodvs in crine ho[min]is.

Ad equum errehet
Man gieng after wege,   zoh sin ros in handon.
do begagenda imo min trohtin   mit sinero arngrihte.
"wes, man, gestu?   zu neridestu?"
"waz mag ih riten?   Min ros ist errehet."
"nu ziuhez da bi fiere,   tu rune imo in daz ora,
drit ez an den cesewen fuoz: so wirt imo des erreheten buoz."

Pater noster. et terge crura eius et pedes, dicens "also sciero werde diesemo—cuiuscumque coloris sit, rot, suarz, blanc, ualo, grisel, feh—rosse des erreheten buoz, samo demo got da selbo buozta".

The Bamberg Blood-Charm

Christ and Judas were playing with lances. Holy Christ was wounded in the side. Then he took his thumb and pressed it upon it. Then the blood stopped, as the waters of the Jordan stopped when Saint John baptized Christ the Saviour in it. Do that for your healing.
Christ was wounded here below.   Of this heaven came to know.
It bled not and it did not sting,   nor was there any poisoning.
That time was very good.   May this wound be healed of blood!

In the name of Jesus Christ. Do that for your healing. *Three Our Fathers, then add three more.* I conjure you by the holy five wounds. Let this wound be healed. *Through the Father +, the Son + and the Holy Spirit +. Let it be. Let it be. Amen.*

For nose-bleeds
Christ and John   went to the Jordan.
Christ said: "stand still, Jordan river,   until I and John have passed over."
As the Jordan then stood,   so may stand *N's* own blood.
Say this three times and each time tie a knot in the man's hair

For equine stiffness
A man went on his way   leading his horse on a rein.
He was met by Our Lord   in His great mercy.
"Why walk you by the side   why do you not ride?"
"How can I ride?   My horse has the stiffness."
"Just take it to you there   and whisper in its ear,
Step on its right foot   and the stiffness will be made good."

Our Father. Then rub its leg and foot, saying: just as quickly may this horse (*of whichever colour it may be*, chestnut, black, dun, grey or piebald) be cured of stiffness, as the Lord cured one the same way.

Lorscher Bienensegen

Kirst, imbi ist hucze!   Nu fliuc du, uihu minaz, hera,
fridu frono in godes munt,   heim zi comonne gisunt.
Sizi, sizi, bina: inbot dir sancte Maria.
Hurolob nihabe du: zi holce nifluc du,
noh du mir nindrinnes,   noh du mir nintuuinnest.
sizi uilu stillo,   uuirki godes uuillon.

Ad signandum domum contra diabolum
Uuola, uuiht, taz tu uueist,   taz tu uuiht heizist,
Taz tu neuueist noch nechanst   cheden chnospinci.

Trierer Spruch wider den Teufel

Nu vuill ih bidan den rihchan crist the mannelihches chenist [ist],
ther den divvel gibant;   in sinen namon uuill ih gan,
nu vuil ih then ureidon   slahan mit ten colbon.

Trierer Reimspruch

Nisal nieman   then diubal uorhtan,
uuanda her nemach manne scada sin, iz nihengi imo use druhtin.

The Lorsch Bee-Charm

Lord Christ, the bees are away!   Now fly, my little beasts to me
in the peace of the Lord   come safely homeward
Stay, bees, stay,   you are commanded by Our Lady.
You have no leave!   You may not fly to the trees,
nor may you flee,   nor get away from me.
Stay very, very still,   and do God's will.

To protect the house against the devil
It's good that you know, evil devil, that you, devil, are called evil,
and that you can't know and can't say: "chnospinci."

Verse from Trier against the Devil

Now shall I hold Lord Christ in my mind,   who is the saviour
of all mankind,
who bound the devil in chains.   I shall go forth in his name.
Now shall I the evil one   with rods belabour and strike down.

Couplet from Trier

No-one should fear   the devil here
He can cause no harm to man   unless Our Lord says he can.

5

Otfrid of Weissenburg

As stressed in the introduction, Otfrid (Otfried) is the most important figure in Old High German poetry. He studied in Fulda under Hrabanus Maurus probably in the 830s. Presumably he was born at the start of the ninth century, and he spent his life mostly as a monk and schoolmaster at the monastery of Weissenburg in what is now Alsace (Wissembourg). We assume that he died in around 870. From the dates of people mentioned in the dedicatory pieces attached to the work we can establish that his Gospel-poem was composed between 863 and 870. Otfrid's lists of firsts is impressive: the first named poet, the first to produce a book of poetry as a coherent entity in its own right, in a fine manuscript which was re-copied. It survives in three full and one fragmentary manuscript, one of them adapted from the South Rhenish Franconian dialect of the original into Bavarian. His work is in over seven thousand end-rhymed long-lines, rhymed verse (a feature of Latin hymns) establishing itself in place of the Germanic alliterative form. It is set in strophes, usually of two of the two-stress long-lines, and this is indicated in the manuscripts by red capitals. The chapters of the five books into which it is divided have Latin headings, these are listed in tables of contents, and there are comments in Latin at the side, so that the dominant Latin culture in which it appeared is never far away.

Otfrid tells the story of the Gospels in five books so that, he says, mankind's impure five senses can be countered by the four-square number of the gospels. Otfrid's presentation is not just narrative, however, but includes interpretations according to the medieval method of biblical exegesis, by which every biblical verse was capable of four interpretative approaches. There are literal (explaining what did or what must have actually happened); tropological or moral (deriving a moral precept for the use of mankind); typological or allegorical (linking the two parts of the Bible); and anagogical (looking towards the end of things). Otfrid either incorporates such interpretation without comment, or signals it with an inserted sub-heading (*mystice, spiritaliter, moraliter*, "symbolic," "spiritual," "moral"), or develops interpretations as chapters in their own right. The first book covers the nativity, the second and third the miracles, the fourth the passion, the last the resurrection, ascension and end of the world.

Before the work starts there are three prefatory sections: dedicatory poems to Ludwig the German, king of the East Franks (Otfrid thinks of himself as a Frank and of his language as Frankish) and to Solomon, Bishop of Constance, both of them acrostic and telestich (that is, with the first letter and the last of each two-line strophe spelling out a message). Matching these at the conclusion is another dedicatory piece in the same form to two monks of St Gallen. Between the first two dedications (all of which have numerical patterns as well) is a letter in Latin to Liutbert, Archbishop of Mainz from 863–9. This letter explains Otfrid's decision to undertake such a patently unusual task as composing in German; it explains about rhymes and reads in places like an apology for the fact that German is not the same as Latin; genders do not match, there are different scribal conventions, and Otfrid regrets that he therefore has to give way to barbarous solecisms. Very different and more positive nationalistic reasons are given in the first chapter of the first book: the Franks are just as good as anyone else and better than many, so why shouldn't there be a Gospel-poem in their language?

Much of the work depends on what we might now call artifice rather than art. Otfrid uses highly complex number patterns throughout, matching words to those of the bible texts, using repeated multiples of lines and other patterns. This has been much studied in the secondary literature. Medieval number symbolism has a complexity all of its own, and it would be very difficult to convey many aspects of the work as a whole, even in a full translation. Of the three full manuscripts, the first, now in Vienna, (V), is from Weissenburg, and Otfrid's own hand is discernible in it, so that we come closer to him than to any other early German writer. The second manuscript, now in Heidelberg (P = Palatine) is a copy, and that now in Munich (M)—originally from Freising—is in Bavarian. The fragmentary codex is referred to as D, *discissus*, cut up.

Otfrid was not the first to attempt such a Gospel poem, of course. There is a Latin tradition, and perhaps more significantly, he knew an Old Low German (Old Saxon) Gospel-poem, *The Heliand* "The Saviour." It is of similar length, also with exegetical additions to the narrative, but it is Germanic alliterative verse, whereas Otfrid uses, of course, the Latinate rhymed form. See *Heliand und Genesis*, ed. Otto Behaghel, 10th ed. by Burkhard Taeger (Tübingen: Niemeyer, 1996); modern German version by Felix Genzmer, *Heliand* (Stuttgart: Reclam, 1966); English prose version by G. Ronald Murphy, *The Heliand: The Saxon Gospel* (Oxford: Oxford University Press, 1992). For studies comparing the two (and with other biblical texts), see Belkin, pp. 44–6 in the bibliography section below.

Since the *Evangelienbuch* is such a substantial work, space dictates that only a small sample may be offered here. The opening German declaration of why Otfrid undertook the work is important in its own right, in spite of the difficulties of his learned and technical play with metrical units, time, ages, and possibly even hexameters, and his curious link between the Franks and Alexander the Great. The story of the arrival of the wise men is exemplary, since it has an allegorical passage within the narrative (which has a more recent parallel in the Christmas carol "We Three Kings"), and then a separate moral interpretation based on the idea of the *patria paradisi*—that mankind lost its real home with the fall of Adam and Eve. His impressive complaint against mankind's exile was highlighted already in a study in 1874 of early Germanic Christian poetry (see Hammerich in the final bibliography II, and also my *Old High German Literature*, where I offer an explication of the two passages). Otfrid's version of the Lord's Prayer from Book II is of separate interest and is taken here from a longer section on the need to pray "with few words" (II, XXI, 15–18; Matthew 6:7). The final piece, from the fifth book, looks at the day of judgement from the biblical Apocalypse.

The first major scholarly edition was that by Johann Kelle in 1856, and there are editions of the text from all of the manuscripts, V being the most important: *Otfrids Evangelienbuch*, ed. Oskar Erdmann (Halle/S.: Waisenhaus, 1882), which was continued by Edward Schröder. The text here is from the sixth edition of Erdmann by Ludwig Wolff (Tübingen: Niemeyer, 1973). There is a more recent edition of the Vienna manuscript by Wolfgang Kleiber: *Otfrid von Weissenburg, Evangelienbuch*, 2 vols. (Tübingen: Niemeyer, 2006). The Heidelberg manuscript was edited by Paul Piper, *Otfrids Evangelienbuch* (Paderborn: Schöningh, 1880), and more recently, together with the fragmentary codex, by Wolfgang Kleiber, *Otfrid von Weissenburg: Evangelienbuch. I: Edition nach der Heidelberger Handschrift P (Codex Pal. Lat. 52) und der Handschrift D (Codex Discissus: Bonn, Berlin/Krakau Wolfenbüttel)*. (Tübingen: Niemeyer, 2004). The Freising version is edited by Karin Pivernetz, *Otfrid von Weissenburg: Das 'Evangelienbuch' in der Überlieferung der Freisinger Hanschrift*, 2 vols. (Göppingen: Kümmerle, 2000). There is an ongoing translation into modern German by Heiko Hartmann, *Otfrid von Weissenburg: Evangelienbuch* (Herne: Verlag für Wissenschaft und Kunst, 2005, 2014–), and a selection with the original and a modern German translation by Gisela Vollmann-Profe, *Otfrid von Weissenburg, Evangelienbuch* (Stuttgart: Reclam, 1987), which also has a

German translation of the Latin letter to Liutbert. She analyses it in detail in her useful *Kommentar*.

Translating rhyme is always a challenge. Of course, the rhymes are sometimes assonances (*pad/straza*), or are just on final unstressed syllables (*ferti/zeigonti*), and occasionally the half lines end with the same word (I, xvii, 43). In the *mystice* section here (I, xviii), incidentally, the formulaic-looking line 9 alliterates rather than rhymes. In Book V, xix, lines 11 and 55 (part of the refrain) are in the original not *quite* the same as line 41, but I have made them uniform. The final refrain line 63 varies it again, but this can at least be signalled. One can, finally, only salute Otfrid for rhyming *Persi* "Persians" with *uuirs si* "be worse" in I, I, 86, but it defies imitation.

The secondary bibliography is again massive, but there is in this case a published bibliography by Johanna Belkin down to 1975, and also a collection of important essays. I have listed otherwise only a few of the more important large-scale studies (it must be admitted that they are for the most part very detailed indeed), plus a couple of articles of interest.

Archibald, Linda. *Cur scriptor hunc librum theotisce dictaverit: The Educational Purpose of Otfrid's Evangelienbuch*. University of Stirling: Doctoral Dissertation, 1989.

Belkin, Johanna and Jürgen Meier. *Bibliographie zu Otfrid von Weissenburg und zur altsächsischen Bibeldichtung*. Berlin: Schmidt, 1975.

Ernst, Ulrich. *Der Liber Evangeliorum Otfrids von Weissenburg*. Cologne and Vienna: Böhlau, 1975.

Hartmann, Reinildis. *Allegorisches Wörterbuch zu Otfrieds von Weissenburg Evangeliendichtung*. Munich: Fink, 1975.

Haubrichs, Wolfgang. *Ordo als Form*. Tübingen: Niemeyer, 1969.

Hellgardt, Ernst. *Die exegetischen Quellen von Otfrids Evangelienbuch*. Tübingen: Niemeyer, 1981.

Kleiber, Wolfgang. *Otfrid von Weissenburg. Untersuchung zur handschriftlichen Überlieferung und Studien zum Aufbau des Evangelienbuches*. Berne and Munich: Francke, 1971.

Kleiber, Wolfgang. *Otfrid von Weissenburg*. Darmstadt: Wissenschaftliche Buchgesellschaft, 1978 (collection of essays).

McKenzie, Donald A. *Otfrid von Weissenburg: Narrator or Commentator?* Stanford: Stanford University Press, 1946.

Magoun, Francis P. "Otfrid's *Ad Liutbertum*." *PMLA* 58 (1943): 869–890.

Patzlaff, Rainer. *Otfrid von Weissenburg und die mittelalterliche versus-Tradition*. Tübingen: Niemeyer, 1975.

Swinburne, Hilda. "Numbers in Otfrid's 'Evangelienbuch'." *Modern Language Review* 52 (1957): 195–202.

Vollmann-Profe, Gisela. *Kommentar zu Otfrids Evangelienbuch: Teil I: Widmungen, Buch I, i–xi*. Bonn: Habelt, 1976.

I, 1

CUR SCRIPTOR HUNC LIBRUM THEOTISCE DICTAVERIT.

Was liuto filu in flize,   in managemo agaleize,
   sie thaz in scrip gicleiptin,   thaz sie iro namon breittin;
Sie thes in io gilicho   flizzun guallicho,
   in buachon man gimeinti   thio iro chuanheiti.
Tharana datun sie ouh thaz duam: ougdun iro wisduam,   5
   ougdun iro cleini   in thes tihtonnes reini.
Iz ist al thuruh not   so kleino giredinot,
   (iz dunkal eigun funtan,   zisamane gibuntan),
Sie ouh in thiu gisagetin,   thaz then thio buah nirsmahetin,
   joh wol er sih firwesti,   then lesan iz gilusti.   10
Zi thiu mag man ouh ginoto   managero thioto
   hiar namon nu gizellen   joh suntar ginennen.
Sar Kriachi joh Romani   iz machont so gizami,
   iz machont sie al girustit,   so thih es wola lustit;
Sie machont iz so rehtaz   joh so filu slehtaz,   15
   iz ist gifuagit al in ein,   selp so helphantes bein.
Thie dati man giscribe: theist mannes lust zi libe;
   nim gouma thera dihta: thaz hursgit thina drahta.
Ist iz prosun slihti: thaz drenkit thih in rihti;
   odo metres kleini: theist gouma filu reini.   20
Sie duent iz filu suazi,   joh mezent sie thie fuazi,
   thie lengi joh thie kurti,   theiz gilustlichaz wurti.
Eigun sie iz bithenkit,   thaz sillaba in ni wenkit,
   sies alleswio ni ruachent,   ni so thie fuazi suachent;
Joh allo thio ziti   so zaltun sie bi noti,   25
   iz mizit ana baga   al io sulih waga.
Yrfurbent sie iz reino   joh harto filu kleino,

I, 1

Why the writer composed this book in German

Many people have earnestly   and with great facility
   tried to write things down   and thereby gain renown,
Equally they   worked vigorously
   so that in books you might read   of all their bold deeds.
To add to their fame   their wisdom was made plain
   and their skills made plain to see   in their fine poetry.
Everything had to be   presented perfectly
   (demanding in sense,   ramified and intense),
In their style it was their aim   that their books were not disdained,
   but would be good indeed   for those who chose to read.
In this context, then,   many races of men
   can here be named   and singled out for fame.
Greeks and Romans as well   have such great skill,
   they write so perfectly   as one wants it to be.
Their work is so neat   and the sense so complete,
   that the whole seems to be   as smooth as ivory.
The deeds of which they write   give everyone delight;
   for literature learn to care   and you will become more aware.
Prose, clear and smooth,   will give refreshment to you,
   and metre, for sure   gives a pleasure most pure.
Poets' work is so sweet   using metrical feet,
   both long and short too,   to give joy to you.
They are always aware   every syllable is there,
   and their eye is ever on   the metrical form.
Each unit and beat   is always complete
   without going astray,   as if it were weighed,
And the work is polished   and finely finished,

selb so man thuruh not   sinaz korn reinot.
Ouh selbun buah frono   irreinont sie so scono;
  thar lisist scona gilust   ana theheiniga akust.   30
Nu es filu manno inthihit,   in sina zungun scribit,
  joh ilit, er gigahe,   thaz sinaz io gihohe:
Wanana sculun Frankon   einon thaz biwankon,
  ni sie in frenkisgon biginnen,   sie gotes lob singen?
Nist si so gisungan,   mit regulu bithuungan: 35
  si habit thoh thia rihti   in sconeru slihti.
Ili thu zi note,   theiz scono thoh gilute,
  joh gotes wizod thanne   tharana scono helle;
Thaz tharana singe,   iz scono man ginenne;
  in themo firstantnisse   wir gihaltan sin giwisse;   40
Thaz laz thir wesan suazi: so mezent iz thie fuazi,
  zit joh thiu regula;   so ist gotes selbes brediga.
Wil thu thes wola drahton,   thu metar wolles ahton,
  in thina zungun wirken duam,   joh sconu vers wolles duan:
Il io gotes willen   allo ziti irfullen,   45
  so scribent gotes thegana   in frenkisgon thie regula;
In gotes gibotes suazi   laz gangan thine fuazi,
  ni laz thir zit thes ingan: theist sconi fers sar gidan;
Dihto io thaz zi noti   theso sehs ziti,
  thaz thu thih so girustes,   in theru sibuntuu girestes.   50
Thaz Kristes wort uns sagetun   joh druta sine uns zelitun,
  bifora lazu ih iz al,   so ih bi rehtemen scal;
Wanta sie iz gisungun   harto in edilzungun,
  mit gote iz allaz riatun,   in werkon ouh giziartun.
Theist suazi joh ouh nuzzi   inti lerit unsih wizzi,   55
  himilis gimacha,   bi thiu ist thaz ander racha.
Ziu sculun Frankon, so ih quad,   zi thiu einen wesan ungimah,
  thie liut es wiht ni dualtun,   thie wir hiar oba zaltun?
Sie sint so sama chuani,   selb so thie Romani;
  ni tharf man thaz ouh redinon, thaz Kriachi in thes giwidaron. 60
Sie eigun in zi nuzzi   so samalicho wizzi,
  in felde joh in walde   so sint sie sama balde;

just as carefully done   as they grade the best corn.
Holy Scripture as well   they present with great skill,
    to be read with delight   with no errors in sight.
Since so many have begun   to write in their own tongue,
    are eager to write down   matters of their own,
Why should the Franks alone   leave it undone,
    nor in Frankish begin   God's praises to sing.
That tongue is unused   to the metrical rules,
    but still it can be   made to fit beautifully.
You need only ensure   that it sounds fine and pure,
    and God's laws would be   voiced beautifully,
So that what you there sing   would be a fine thing,
    and our understanding   would be made firm and strong.
Let God's word be sweet: mark the metrical feet
    and the patterns and form   —it will be like God's sermon.
If you have in mind   the right metres to find,
    in your tongue to indite   and fine verses write,
Into God's guidance sweet   direct your own feet,
    from the rules do not stray   —fine verse will come that way.
Write, if you can,   through the six measures of man,
    so you are fitted best   in the seventh to rest.
Christ's words to all men   and what his disciples taught then
    I place first and foremost,   as indeed I must,
For what they had to say   was fine in every way,
    guided always by God   who enhanced what they did.
It is sweet and useful   and imparts wisdom too,
    a heavenly thing,   not like other writings.
Why should Franks, as I asked,   not be up to this task,
    when the others I named   have done it all the same?
Franks are just as bold   as the Romans of old,
    nor can anyone say   that the Greeks were better in that way.
The Franks use and they own   just as much wisdom,
    in the fields and the woods   they are also as good,
Great wealth they possess   and battle-prowess,
    swift to take up weapons   are their warriors, each one.

Rihiduam ginuagi   joh sint ouh filu kuani,
   zi wafane snelle   so sint thie thegana alle.
Sie buent mit giziugon   (joh warun io thes giwon)   65
   in guatemo lante;   bi thiu sint sie unscante.
Iz ist filu feizit,   (harto ist iz giweizit)
   mit managfalten ehtin;   nist iz bi unsen frehtin.
Zi nuzze grebit man ouh thar   er inti kuphar,
   joh bi thia meina   isine steina;   70
Ouh tharazua fuagi   silabar ginuagi,
   joh leseut thar in lante   gold in iro sante.
Sie sint fastmuate   zi managemo guate,
   zi manageru nuzzi;   thaz duent in iro wizzi.
Sie sint filu redie   sih fianton zirrettinne;   75
   ni gidurrun sies biginnan,   sie eigun se ubarwunnan.
Liut sih in nintfuarit,   thaz iro lant ruarit,
   ni sie bi iro guati   in thionon io zi noti;
Joh mennisgon alle,   ther se iz ni untarfalle,
   (ih weiz, iz got worahta)   al eigun se iro forahta.   80
Nist liut, thaz es biginne,   thaz widar in ringe;
   in eigun sie iz firmeinit,   mit wafanon gizeinit.
Sie lertun sie iz mit swerton,   nalas mit then worton,
   mit speron filu wasso;   bi thiu forahten sie se noh so.
Ni si thiot, thaz thes gidrahte,   in thiu iz mit in fehte,   85
   thoh Medi iz sin joh Persi,   nub in es thiu wirs si.
Las ih iu in alawar   in einen buachon (ih weiz war),
   sie in sibbu joh in ahtu   sin Alexandres slahtu,
Ther worolti so githrewita,   mit suertu sia al gistrewita
   untar sinen hanton   mit filu herten banton;   90
Joh fand in theru redinu,   thaz fon Macedoniu
   ther liut in giburti   gisceidiner wurti.
Nist untar in thaz thulte,   thaz kuning iro walte,
   in worolti niheine,   ni si thie sie zugun heime;
Odo in erdringe   ander thes beginne   95
   in thiheinigemo thiete,   thaz ubar sie gibiete.
Thes eigun sie io nuzzi   in snelli joh in wizzi;

They have all that they need   (and have long done so, indeed)
   in a land that is rich   (they can be proud of it).
The land can provide,   as is known far and wide,
   many things from the earth   far more than we deserve.
For use, men can mine here   copper and iron ore,
   and as I can tell,   fine crystal as well.
Added to these must be   silver in quantity,
   and also in our land,   gold from the rivers' sand.
Franks are resolute   in many good pursuits
   that are of great value,   as their wisdom helps them do.
They are always ready   to face an enemy;
   if any should dare,   they are driven from there.
No people can   in the neighbouring lands
   escape their superiority;   their subjects they must be,
And all other nations   save those beyond the ocean
   (as I know God foresaw)   hold them in great awe.
No folk alive   would engage them in strife;
   they have let it be seen   that their weapons are keen.
They taught with their swords,   and not with their words,
   and with many sharp spears   put them in great fear.
No people should think   to engage with the Franks,
   even Medes and Persians   would come off worse then.
I read in a book, too,   and I know it is true,
   that they are of the same race   as Alexander the Great,
Who threatened the whole world,   conquered it with his sword,
   kept it all in his hands   with iron-strong bands.
I read in the same place   that the Macedonian race
   differ by birth   from all others on earth,
None of them tolerating   that they be ruled by a king,
   whoever it might be,   who was not from their country,
Or that on earth any man   should even begin
   (from any people at all)   to put them under his rule.
The king's value to them   is in strength and wisdom,
   they have no-one to fear   if their king is safely there.
He is brave above all,   as befits a noble lord,

ni intratent sie niheinan,   unz se inan eigun heilan.
Er ist gizal ubar al,   io so edilthegan skal,
   wiser inti kuani;   thero eigun sie io ginuagi.   100
Weltit er githiuto   managero liuto,
   joh ziuhit er se reine   selb so sine heime.
Ni sint thie imo ouh derien,   in thiu nan Frankon werien;
   thie snelli sine irbiten,   thaz sie nan umbiriten.
Wanta allaz thaz sies thenkent,   sie iz al mit gote wirkent;   105
   ni duent sies wiht in noti   ana sin girati.
Sie sint gotes worto   flizig filu harto,
   thaz sie thaz gilerncn,   thaz in thia buah zellen;
Thaz sie thes biginnen,   iz uzana gisingen,
   joh sie iz ouh irfullen   mit mihilemo willen.   110
Gidan ist es nu redina,   thaz sie sint guate thegana,
   ouh gote thiononti alle   joh wisduames folle.
Nu will ih scriban unser heil,   evangeliono deil,
   so wir nu hiar bigunnun,   in frenkisga zungun;
Thaz sie ni wesen eino   thes selben adeilo,   115
   ni man in iro gizungi   Kristes lob sungi;
Joh er ouh iro worto   gilobot werde harto,
   ther sie zimo holeta,   zi giloubon sinen ladota.
Ist ther in iro lante   iz alleswio nintstante,
   in ander gizungi   firneman iz ni kunni: 120
Hiar hor er io zi guate,   waz got imo gibiete,
   thaz wir imo hiar gisungun   in frenkisga zungun.
Nu frewen sih es alle,   so wer so wola wolle,
   joh so wer si hold in muate   Frankono thiote,
Thaz wir Kriste sungun   in unsera zungun,   125
   joh wir ouh thaz gilebetun,   in frenkisgon nan lobotun!

wise and in battle keen have their kings ever been.
The king has under his rule many other folk too
 and he treats them as well as his own people.
No one can be harmed whom the Franks guard,
 attacks are set aside when they to their defence ride.
 For in all the Franks do, God is with them too,
 no undertaking is done without Him.
With the word of the Lord they are in great accord,
 and try to learn well what the Bible can tell,
So that there are parts they can recite by heart,
 and they try to fulfil what is said with good will.
I have now made plain that they are all good thanes,
 who serve God each one, and are full of wisdom.
Of our salvation I'll tell using the Gospels,
 so we may here engage in the Frankish language,
So that they are not left alone and bereft,
 and that in their own tongue Christ's praise may be sung,
And that their own words will give praise to the Lord,
 Who has called them to Him, in faith gathered them in.
If someone in their land does not understand
 the other tongues of men, and cannot take it in,
Here he may hear the good word of what God has offered,
 which here to him shall be sung in the Frankish tongue.
Now may rejoice all who are of good will,
 and all who wish well to the Frankish people,
That of Christ shall be sung in our own tongue,
 and we are granted our wish to praise Him in Frankish.

I, xvii

DE STELLA ET ADVENTU MAGORUM.

Nist man nihein in worolti,   thaz saman al irsageti,
  wio manag wuntar wurti   zi theru druhtines giburti.
 Bi thiu thaz ih irdualta,   thar forna ni gizalta,
  scal ih iz mit willen   nu sumaz hiar irzellen.
Tho druhtin Krist giboran ward   (thes mera ih sagen nu ni tharf), 5
  thaz blidi worolt wurti   theru saligun giburti;
Thaz ouh gidan wurti,   si in ewon ni firwurti
  (iz was iru anan henti,   tho det es druhtin enti):
Tho quamun ostana in thaz lant,   thie irkantun sunnun fart,
  sterrono girusti;   thaz warun iro listi.   10
Sie eiscotun thes kindes   sar io thes sinthes,
  joh kundtun ouh tho mari,   thaz er ther kuning wari.
Warun fragenti,   war er giboran wurti,
  joh batun io zi noti,   man in iz zeigoti.
Sie zaltun seltsani   joh zeichan filu wahi,   15
  wuntar filu hebigaz,   wanta er ni horta man thaz,
Thaz io fon magadburti   man giboran wurti;
  inti ouh zeichan sin sconaz   in himile so scinaz.
Sagetun thaz sie gahun   sterron einan sahun
  joh datun filu mari,   thaz er sin wari.   20
"Wir sahun sinan sterron,   thoh wir thera burgi irron,
  joh quamun thaz wir betotin,   ginada sino thigitin.
Ostar filu ferro   so scein uns ouh ther sterro;
  ist iaman hiar in lante,   es iawiht thoh firstante?
Gistirri zaltun wir io,   ni sahun wir nan er io;   25
  bi thiu birun wir nu gieinot,   er niwan kuning zeinot.
So scribun uns in lante   man in worolti alte;

I, xvii

On the star and the arrival of the wise men

No-one in the world at all   could relate in full
   every mystery   seen at Our Lord's nativity.
Since there was so much more   I could have said before,
   I shall try without fail   to tell you one tale.
When Our Lord Christ was born   —of that I need say no more—
   and there was joy on earth   at this blessed birth,
For, since this came to be,   we were not doomed eternally
   (the time was now at hand   when God saved us from being damned),
Men came from the east to that land   who knew how the sun ran,
   knew the place of the stars   —that skill was theirs.
To find the baby   they set out on their way,
   the great news to bring   that the child was a king.
They asked all around   where the new-born could be found,
   and asked everywhere   to be shown the way there.
They said there had been   wonders and signs seen,
   manifestations   unknown to all nations,
That a virgin mild   had borne a child,
   and that a sign bright   shone in the heavens at night.
They said they had hurried there   when they saw a star,
   and knew by this wondrous thing   that the star was for him.
"We saw his star,   of the place we are unsure
   but we came to worship him,   and his grace to obtain.
From the East so far   shone the light of his star,
   is there anyone in this land   that can understand?
We have long studied star-lore   but not seen this star before,
   we agree on the meaning: it must show a new king.
Prophets wrote of it so   in our land long ago,

thaz ir uns ouh gizellet,   wio iz iwo buah singent."
So thisu wort tho gahun   then kuning anaquamun,
   hintarquam er harto   thero selbero worto   30
Joh manniliches houbit   ward es thar gidruabit;
   gihortun ungerno,   thaz wir nu niazen gerno.
Thie buachara ouh tho thare   gisamanota er sare,
   sie was er fragenti,   war Krist giboran wurti.
Er sprah zen ewarton   selben thesen worton;   35
   gab armer joh ther richo   antwurti gilicho.
Thia burg nantun se sar,   in festiz datun alawar
   mit worton, then er thie altun   forasagon zaltun.
So er giwisso thar bifand,   war druhtin Krist giboran ward,
   thaht er sar in festi   mihilo unkusti.   40
Zi imo er ouh tho ladota   thie wisun man, theih sageta,
   mit in gistuant er thingon   joh filu halingon.
Thia zit eiscota er fon in,   so ther sterro giwon was queman zi in;
   bat sie iz ouh biruahtin,   bi thaz selba kind irsuahtin.
"Giduet mih," quad er, "anawart   bi thes sterren fart;   45
   so faret, eiscot thare   bi thaz kind sare!
Sin eiscot iogilicho   joh filu giwaralicho,
   sliumo duet ouh thanne   iz mir zi wizzanne.
Ih willu faran beton nan   (so riet mir filu manag man),
   thaz ih tharzua githinge   joh imo ouh geba bringe."   50
Long ther wenego man,   er wankota thar filu fram;
   er wolta nan irthuesben   joh uns thia fruma irlesgen.
Thaz imbot sie gihortun   joh iro ferti iltun;
   yrscein in sar tho ferro   ther seltsano sterro.
Sie blidtun sih es gahun,   sar sie nan gisahun,   55
   joh filu frawalicho   sin wartetun gilicho,
Leit er sie tho scono,   thar was thaz kind frono,
   mit sineru ferti   was er iz zeigonti.
Thaz hus sie tho gisahun   joh sar tharain quamun;
   thar was ther sun guater   mit sineru muater.   60
Fialun sie tho framhald,   thes guates warun sie bald,
   thaz kind sie thar tho betotun   joh huldi sino thigitun.

therefore tell us please   what your books say of this."
These words of theirs   soon reached the king's ears,
    and what they had said   filled him with dread,
and many men more   were also troubled sore,
    and hated to hear   what to us is so dear.
The king called upon   his scholars, every one,
    and quizzed them thereon,   where the Christ would be born.
He told the priests, too   about this same news,
    and these, low or high,   gave him the same reply.
They told him the town's name   and supported their claim
    with words once foretold   by the prophets of old.
When he had learned   where Christ was born,
    thoughts came to his mind   of a most evil kind.
He to his palace called   the wise men of whom I told,
    and had a discussion   with them in secret session.
He asked of them   when the star first came to them,
    and told them to go   and to seek that child now.
He said:"Tell me true   where the star leads you,
    go there indeed,   find the child with all speed!
Seek him diligently   and very carefully,
    then very quickly   bring the news back to me.
I wish to go and worship him   —on the advice of many men—
    that I my hopes may tell,   and bring him gifts as well."
The wretched man was lying!   He had in mind no such thing!
    He wanted to kill the boy   and so our salvation destroy.
They listened to what he had to say   then hurried on their way,
    then there appeared from afar   that unusual star.
It cheered them greatly   that star to see,
    and with much rejoicing   followed it again.
It led them wonderfully   to the child so holy,
    by its course in the sky   it showed the way from on high,
They saw the house   and went in at once,
    found the son so dear   with his mother there.
They fell down in that place,   hoping for his grace,
    the child worshipping   and wanting his blessing.

Indatun sie tho thare   thaz iro dreso sare,
   rehtes sie githahtun,   thaz sie imo geba brahtun;
Myrrun inti wirouh   joh gold scinantaz ouh,   65
   geba filu mara;   sie suahtun sine wara.

Mystice

Ih sagen thir thaz in wara,   sie mohtun bringan mera;
   thiz was sus gibari   theiz geistlichaz wari.
Kundtun sie uns thanne,   so wir firnemen alle,
   gilouba in girihti   in theru wuntarlichun gifti: 70
Thaz er urmari   uns ewarto wari,
   ouh kuning in giburti   joh bi unsih dot wurti.

Sie wurtun slafente   fon engilon gimanote,
   in droume sie in zelitun   then weg sie faran scoltun;
Thaz sie ouh thes ni thahtin,   themo kuninge sih nahtin,   75
   noh gikundtin thanne   thia fruma themo manne.
Tho fuarun thie ginoza   andara straza
   harto ilente   zi eiginemo lante.

They laid before him   their precious things,
    for they had rightly thought   that gifts should be brought:
Myrrh and frankincense   and gold bright and intense,
    gifts most rare.   They sought his truth there.

Spiritual interpretation
I tell you for sure   although they could have brought more,
    this was right to do   —it was spiritually true.
They make it clear,   as we all must be aware,
    for us to believe as we ought   by the wonderful gifts they brought:
That the great one would be   a priest for you and me,
    was by birth royal   and would die for us all.

When they were sleeping   the angels gave a warning,
    in a dream they were shown   which road to take home,
Never even thinking   of approaching the king,
    nor passing on then   the great news to that man.
The Magi then set out   by a different route
    as fast as could be   to their own country.

I, xviii

MYSTICE.

Manot unsih thisu fart, thaz wir es wesen anawart,
 wir unsih ouh biruachen inti eigan lant suachen.
Thu ni bist es, wan ih, wis: thaz lant thaz heizit paradis;
 ih meg iz lobon harto, ni girinnit mih thero worto.
Thoh mir megi lidolih sprechan wortogilih,   5
 ni mag ih thoh mit worte thes lobes queman zi ente.
Ni bist es io giloubo, selbo thu iz ni scowo;
 ni mahtu iz ouh noh thanne yrzellen iomanne.
Thar ist lib ana tod, lioht ana finstri,
 engilichaz kunni joh ewinigo wunni.   10
Wir eigun iz firlazan; thaz mugun wir io riazan
 joh zen inheimon io emmizigen weinon.
Wir fuarun thanana noti thuruh ubarmuati,
 yrspuan unsih so stillo ther unser muatwillo.
Ni woltun wir gilos sin, harto wegen wir es scin,   15
 nu riazen elilente in fremidemo lante;
Nu ligit uns umbitherbi thaz unser adalerbi,
 ni niazen sino guati; so duat uns ubarmuati!
Tharben wir nu, lewes, liebes filu manages,
 joh thulten hiar nu noti bittero ziti.   20
Nu birun wir mornente mit seru hiar in lante,
 in managfalten wunton bi unseren sunton;
Arabeiti manego sint uns hiar io garawo,
 ni wollen heim wison wir wenegon weison.
Wolaga elilenti, harto bistu herti,   25
 thu bist harto filu suar, thaz sagen ih thir in alawar.
Mit arabeitin werbent thie heiminges tharbent;

I, xviii

Spiritual interpretation

In the Magi's return   is a lesson to learn,
    to consider how we   may seek our own country.
I think you may not be so wise   as to know our land is Paradise.
    I could praise it fulsomely   but my word-skills fail me.
If every part of my body   could find words equally,
    still my words never could   give it the praise it should.
You would not believe me   unless you saw directly,
    and could not, even then   describe it to men.
There is life without death,   light without darkness,
    the angels' company   and everlasting felicity.
The land that we left,   we must ever regret,
    and for it, our home,   we must ever greatly mourn.
We were set outside   because of our pride,
    we were led astray silently   by our impetuosity.
We would not obey,   and see our punishment today:
    into sad exile banned,   in a strange land.
We now have no chance   of our true inheritance,
    no joy may we share,   our pride drove us from there.
Alas, we must miss   so very much bliss,
    and we have to bear   bitter times here.
Now we suffer misery   here in this country,
    wounded and in pain   because of our sin.
Much toil and fear   lies in wait for us here,
    yet we won't try to return,   we wretched orphans.
Woe, woe to you, exile,   you are the hardest of all trials!
    You are so hard to bear,   I tell you that for sure.
Suffering is the cost   if your homeland is lost

ih haben iz funtan in mir,   ni fand ih liebes wiht in thir;
Ni fand in thir ih ander guat,   suntar rozagaz muat,
   seragaz herza   joh managfalta smerza.   30
Ob uns in muat gigange,   thaz unsih heim lange,
   zi themo lante in gahe   ouh jamar gifahe:
Farames so thie ginoza   ouh andara straza,
   then weg ther unsih wente   zi eiginemo lante.
Thes selben pades suazi   suachit reine fuazi;   35
   si therer situ in manne   ther tharana gange:
Thu scalt haben guati   joh mihilo otmuati,
   in herzen io zi noti   waro karitati;
Dua thir zi giwurti   scono furiburti,
   wis horsam io zi guate,   ni hori themo muate,   40
Innan thines herzen kust   ni laz thir thesa woroltlust,
   fliuh thia geginwerti;   so quimit thir fruma in henti.
Hugi wio ih tharfora quad,   thiz ist ther ander pad;
   gang thesan weg, ih sagen thir ein,   er gileitit thih heim.
So thu thera heimwisti   niuzist mit gilusti,   45
   so bistu gote liober,   ni intratist scadon niamer.

and I have found too   no good things in you.
Nothing in you have I found   but gloom all around,
    most painful heartache,   and much sorrow to take.
If we have in mind   our homeland to find,
    and if homeward again   we are drawn by our pain,
Then, like the Magi,   a new path we must try,
    the way that will lead   to our homeland indeed.
This path's purity   needs footsteps of piety,
    there are things to be done   by those walking thereon:
You must be good inwardly,   have great humility,
    in your heart there should be   true charity.
For your own sake   proper abstinence take,
    in obedience trust,   pay no heed to your lusts.
In the depths of your heart   keep from worldliness apart,
    flee from earthly desires   and the prize shall be yours.
Think about what I have said: this is the *other* path to tread.
    I tell you, if you take this road   it will bring you home.
When you enter your homeland   with all its joys to hand,
    to God you shall be dear   and shall suffer harm no more.

II, xxi, 27–40

(QUOMODO SIT ORANDUM, ET) DE ORATIONE DOMINICA.

Fater unser guato, bist druhtin thu gimyato
 in himilon io hoher, wih si namo thiner.
Biqueme uns thinaz richi, thaz hoha himilrichi,
 thara wir zua io gingen joh emmizigen thingen. 30
Si willo thin hiar nidare, sos er ist ufin himile;
 in erdu hilf uns hiare, so thu engilon duist nu thare.
Thia dagalichun zuhti gib hiut uns mit ginuhti,
 joh follon ouh, theist mera, thines selbes lera.
Sculd bilaz uns allen, so wir ouh duan wollen, 35
 sunta thia wir thenken joh emmizigen wirken.
Ni firlaze unsih thin wara in thes widarwerten fara,
 thaz wir ni missigangen, thara ana ni gifallen.
Losi unsih io thanana, thaz wir sin thine thegana,
 joh mit ginadon thinen then wewon io bimiden. Amen. 40

II, xxi, 27–40

(How to Pray, and) the Lord's Prayer

Our father, so good,   you are our blessed lord
   in heaven's high plain;   hallowed be your name.
May to us be given   your kingdom of heaven,
   to which we ever strive   and much hope there to live.
Your will be done here below   as in heaven just so,
   aid us on earth here,   as you help angels there.
Daily sustenance   give us this day enough,
   and what is worth far more,   all your teachings and lore.
Forgive us all blame   that we may do the same,
   for all our sins of thought   and those that we carry out.
Do not let us fall   into the wicked one's thrall,
   that we do not stray there   and fall into the snare.
Deliver us from evil   that we may be your people,
   that by your grace alone   we escape from all pain.

V, xix

DE DIE JUDICII.

Thes habet er ubar woroltring   gimeinit einaz dagathing,
    thing filu hebigaz,   zi sorganne eigun wir bi thaz.
Thir zellu ih hiar ubarlut: nist niheinig siner drut,
    thes alleswio biginne   ni er queme zi themo thinge.
Quement thara ouh thanne   thie wenegun alle,   5
    thie hiar gidatun follon   then iro muatwillon.
Zi zellenne ist iz suari!   nist ther fon wibe quami
    (es irquimit muat min),   nub er thar sculi sin;
Ni sie sculin herton   thar iro dati renton
    al io giwisso umbiring,   theist filu jamarlichaz thing!   10
      Ward wola in then thingon   thie selbun mennisgon,
        thie thar thoh bigonoto   sint sichor iro dato;
      In thie thoh ubil thanne   nist wiht zi zellenne,
        mit thiu sih thoh biwerien   joh etheswio ginerien!
Wanta es nist laba furdir,   thaz giloubi thu mir,   15
    er wergin megi ingangan   (werd er thar bifangan),
Nub er sculi thuruh not   (werd er thar biredinot)
    thulten thanne in ewon   thes helliwizes wewon.
      Ward wola in then thingon   thie selbun mennisgon,
        thie thar thoh bigonoto   sint sichor iro dato!   20
Weist thu wio bi thia zit   ther gotes forasago quit?
    er zelit bi thaz selba thing,   thaz thar si mihilaz githuing;
In imo man thar lesan mag   theiz ist abulges dag,

V, xix

On the Day of Judgement

God has for the whole world-ring   set a day of reckoning
  A court of great power!   We should all fear that hour.
I tell you as clearly as I can   that there is not a man
  who could do anything   to avoid that accounting.
To it shall also come   those wretches, every one,
  who on earth used to do   what their desires led them to.
To tell this gives me pain!   Every man born of woman
  (my heart shakes with fear!)   will have to appear,
When everyone needs   to account for their deeds
  for sure when they are brought   before that dreadful court.
    Happy is the man   who at that judgement day can
      stand there indeed   confident in his deeds,
    With no wickedness   for him to confess —
      his defence he will have,   and he may be saved.
There is no other way   (believe what I say!);
  if he seeks a way out   he will be caught without doubt,
And if it should be   that he is deemed guilty,
  he will suffer for eternity   hell's misery.
    Happy is the man   who at that judgement day can
      stand there indeed   confident in his deeds,
What did God's prophet say   about this day?
  He says that this judgement   is of fearsome intent;
In his book you may   read of the wrathful day,

arabeito, quisti,   joh managoro angusti.

Thaz ist ouh dag hornes   joh engilliches galmes,   25

    thie blasent hiar in lante,   thaz worolt ufstante;

Theist dag ouh nibulnisses   joh wintesbruti, lewes,

    thiu zuei firwazent thanne   thie suntigon alle;

Hermido ginoto   joh wenagheiti thrato

    (waz mag ih zellen thir hiar mer?) — thes ist ther dag al foller! 30

Lasi thu io thia redina,   wio druhtin threwit thanana?

    thar duat er zi gihugte,   er thanne himil scutte.

Wer ist manno in lante,   ther thanne witharstante,

    thanne er iz zi thiu gifiarit   thaz sih ther himil ruarit;

Thanne er mit giwelti   ist inan faltonti   35

    (queman mag uns thaz in muat!),   so man sinan livol duat.

Nist ther dag sumirih   dagon anderen gilih,

    thaz sar man in githankon   thar megi wiht biwankon;

Giborganero dato   ni pligit man hiar nu thrato,

    sih ougit thar ana wank   ther selbo luzilo githank.   40

        Ward wola mennisgon   in then selben thingon,

            thie thar thoh bigonoto   sint sichor iro dato;

        In thie thoh ubil thanne   nist wiht zi zellenne,

            mit thiu sih thoh biwerien   joh etheswio ginerien!

Ni losent thar in noti   gold noh diuro wati,   45

    ni hilfit gotowebbi thar   noh thaz silabar in war;

Ni mag thar manahoubit   helfan hereren wiht,

    kind noh quena in ware,   sie sorgent iro thare;

Odo iawiht helphan thanne   themo filu richen manne;

    sie sint al ebanreiti   in theru selbun arabeiti.   50

Giwisso thaz ni hiluh thih: thar sorget mannilih bi sih,

    bi sines selbes sela;   nist wiht in thanne mera.

Skalka joh thie riche   thie gent thar al giliche,

of sorrow and tears   and of many fears.
Then the trumpet shall give voice   and the angels make noise,
    so that in all the land   the dead shall upstand.
It will be a day or darkness   and of tempests, alas,
    and they will sweep away then   all sinful men.
Great sorrowing   and much suffering
    (what more can I say?)   — they will fill up that day!
Have you read the word   of the threats of Our Lord?
    His words there are spoken: the firmament shall be broken.
No man in the land   could ever withstand
    when it is God's intent   to break the firmament,
And with His great might   fold and close it up tight,
    (in our hearts we must know!)   as a book might be closed.
The day will be for sure   like no other before
    and there is no way   to escape on that day;
Nor can any man with speed   do any secret deed,
    and his slightest thought   to the light shall be brought.
        Happy is the man   who at that judgement day can
            stand there indeed   confident in his deeds,
        With no wickedness   for him to confess —
            his defence he will have,   and he may be saved.
No ransom can you pay   with gold or fine array,
    rich garments are no use   nor silver, in truth,
Nor can an underling   help his master then,
    nor wife and children for sure   (they have their own cares).
There is nothing that can   assist a very rich man,
    all men are the same   in this hour of pain.
I will not hide what is known: each man must stand alone,
    fear for his own soul   the most important thing of all.
Servants and rich men   will be all equal then,

ni si thie thar bi noti   gifordoront thio guati.
    Ward wola in then thingon   thie selbun mennisgon,   55
      thie thar thoh bigonoto   sint sichor iro dato!
Thar nist miotono wiht   ouh wehsales niawiht,
    thaz iaman thes giwise,   mit wihtu sih irlose;
Ni wari thu io so richi   ubar woroltrichi,
    thoh thu es thar biginnes: ther scaz ist sines sindes.   60
Wanta druhtin ist so guat,   ther thaz urdeili duat;
    er duat iz selbo, ih sagen thir ein,   ander botono nihein;
    Bi thiu ist wola in then thingon   thie selbun mennisgon,
      thie thar thoh bigonoto   sint sichor iro dato;
    In thie thoh ubil thanne   nist wiht zi zellenne,   65
      mit thiu sih thoh biwerien   joh etheswio ginerien!

but some in that hour of need are set apart by their good deeds.
   Happy is the man   who at that judgement day can
     stand there indeed   confident in his deeds,
No ransom or fine   can be used at that time,
  and no-one can pay   to be redeemed in that way.
However great your worth   when you were on earth,
  here nothing can be done —   all your treasures are gone.
For the Lord is so just   that each sentence is passed
  by the Lord God Himself   and by nobody else.
   Happy is the man   who at that judgement day can
    stand there indeed   confident in his deeds,
  With no wickedness   for him to confess —
   his defence he will have,   and he may be saved.

6

Christ and the Samaritan Woman

The biblical story of Christ's encounter with the Samaritan woman is in John 4:6–26, which is the Gospel reading for the Friday after the third Sunday in Lent. The poem, composed around 950 in the Alemannic dialect, is in 31 rhymed long lines. The work was written (not always very clearly, so that some editing has been undertaken over the years) in a manuscript containing a Latin chronicle, now in the Austrian National Library, originally from the monastery of the Reichenau on Lake Constance. In line 8 the woman rather anachronistically says, perhaps for the rhyme, "Christ knows." Otfrid also tells the story in his Gospel book (*Evangelienbuch* II. 14. 1–60), but does so rather more expansively and carefully, with an eye on the spiritual interpretation. The theme is the contrast between the actual and the "living water," and Otfrid has Christ and the woman use different OHG words for "well" as a consistent distinction (see J. Knight Bostock in *Medium Aevum* 16, 1947, 53–57). There is a rather later (thirteenth century) English poem on the theme in 77 lines in Richard Morris, *An Old English Miscellany* (London: Early English Text Society, 1872 = OS 49), pp. 84–6, which provides an interesting comparison.

The text is Steinmeyer XVII, MSD X, Braune XXXIV. Some editors have reversed the order of lines 5 and 6 but Steinmeyer is followed here.

Kolbe, P. R. "Variation in the Old High German Post-Otfridian Poems." *MLN* 28 (1913): 216–217.

Maurer, Friedrich. "Zur Frage nach der Heimat des Gedichtes Christus und die Samariterin." *Zeitschrift für deutsche Philologie* 54 (1929): 175–179.

Pakis, Valentine A. "Sharing vessels with an *Armez Wib*: Jesus and the Samaritan Woman in Medieval Germanic." *Journal of English and Germanic Philology* 104 (2006): 514–527.

Pakis, Valentine A. "Line One of 'Christus und die Samariterin' (ÖNB 515)." *Zeitschrift für deutsche Philologie* 129 (2010): 441–448.

Pezzo, Rafaella del. "Cristo e la Samaritana." *Annali dell'Istituto Orientale di Napoli/Sez. Germ.* 14 (1971): 105–116.

Christus und die Samariterin

Lesen uuir, thaz fuori   ther heilant fartmuodi,
    ze untarne, uuizzun thaz,   er zeinen brunnon kisaz.
Quam fone Samario   ein quena sario
    scephan thaz uuazzer: thanna noh so saz er.
Bat er sih ketrencan   daz uuip, thaz ther thara quam: 5
    uuurbon sina thegana   be sina lipleita.
"Biuuaz kerost thu, guot man,   daz ih thir geba trinkan?
    Ia neniezant, uuizze Christ,   thie Iudon unsera uuist."
"Uuip, obe thu uuissis,   unielih gotes gift ist,
    unte den ercantis,   mit themo du kosotis,   10
    tu batis dir unnen   sines kecprunnen".
"Disiu buzza ist so tiuf,   ze dero ih heimina liuf,
    noh tu ne habis kiscirres,   daz thu thes kiscephes:
    uuar maht thu, guot man,   neman quecprunnan?
Ne bistu liuten kelop   mer than Iacob.   15
    ther gab uns thesan brunnan,   tranc er nan ioh sina man;
    siniu smalenozzer   nuzzon thaz uuazzer."
"Ther trinkit thiz uuazzer,   be demo thurstit inan mer,
    der afar trinchit daz min,   then lazit der durst sin:
    iz sprangot imo'n pruston   in euuon mit luston."   20
"Herro, ih thicho ze dir,   thaz uuazzer gabist du mir,
    daz ih mer ubar tac   ne liufi hera durstac."
"Uuib, tu dih anneuuert,   hole hera dinen uuirt."
    Siu quat, sus libiti,   commen ne hebiti.
"Uueiz ih, daz du uuar segist,   daz du commen ne hebist,   25
    du hebitos er finfe   dir zi uolliste.
    Des mahttu sichure sin: nu hebist enin der nis din."
"Herro, in thir uuigit scin,   daz thu maht [forasago sin]:

Christ and the Woman of Samaria

We read how Our Lord   was weary on the road,
    and at midday (we know that)   by a well he sat.
There came along there   a woman of Samaria
    her water-pot to fill   while he was there still.
He asked that woman   to give him a drink then
    (the disciples had gone   to find provisions).
"Good man, how can you think   I could give you a drink,
    Christ knows that the Jews   do not share our food."
"Woman, if you but knew   what God's gift is to you,
    and if you recognised   who is here before your eyes,
    you would ask water from him   from the living spring."
"This well is a deep one   to which I have come,
    but you have no cup   to take the water up,
    so how can you bring   water from a living spring?
Your fame is not more   than was Jacob's of yore,
    who gave us this well —   from it men drank their fill,
    and their flocks of sheep   also drank deep."
"Whoever drinks this water   thirsts again soon thereafter,
    but whoever drinks mine   will not thirst again,
    for it gives in his breast   always joy of the best."
"Lord, I beseech you   give me that water too,
    so that all through the day   my thirst shall be away."
"Woman, go now quickly,   bring your husband to me."
    She said she lived alone,   husband had she none.
"I know that you speak true,   that no husband have you,
    but you had had five   to support you in life,
    and I tell you for sure   you have one who is not yours."
"Sir, I clearly see,   a prophet you must be.

for uns er giborana   betoton hiar in berega,
Unser altmaga   suohton hia genada: 30
    thoh ir sagant kicorana   thia bita in Hierosol[ima]."

Our people long ago   prayed in these hills, I know.
Our forefathers sought grace   here in this place,
    but you (Jews) say   the chosen in Jerusalem should pray...

83

7

Psalm 138

A liturgical manuscript from Freising (now in Vienna) dating from the early part of the tenth century contains a (very) free rendering of Psalm 138 (139 in the Protestant tradition), not in close biblical order. The text is in 38 rhymed long lines (with some alliteration), arranged with initial capitals into two or three-line strophes. There are some omissions, and the text is problematic in some places, with a few lines difficult to interpret. The rhymes are not always good and one (25) is a simple repetition. Three lines are repeated within the piece, and overall the order is questionable. It has been suggested that the work was written down from memory. The dialect is Bavarian.

The text followed is that in Steinmeyer (XXII), with the strophic arrangement made slightly clearer as in Braune XXXVII, where alternative line-numbering is also provided. It is MSD XIII.

Krogmann, Willy. *Der althochdeutsche "138. Psalm": forschungsgeschichtlicher Überblick und Urfassung.* Hamburg: Wittig, 1973.

Ludwig, Otto. "Der althochdeutsche und der biblische Psalm 138. Ein Vergleich." *Euphorion* 56 (1962): 402–409.

Menhardt, Hermann. "Die Überlieferung des althochdeutschen 138. Psalms." *Zeitschrift für deutsches Altertum* 77 (1940): 76–84.

Willems, Fritz. "Psalm 138 und althochdeutscher Stil." *Deutsche Vierteljahresschrift* 29 (1955): 429–446.

Psalm 138

Uellet ir gihoren   Dauiden den guoton,
   den sinen touginon sin?   Er gruozte sinen trohtin:
Ia gichuri du mih, trohtin,   inte irchennist uuer ih pin,
   fone demo aneginne   uncin an daz enti.
Ne megih in gidanchun   fore dir giuuanchon: 5
   du irchennist allo stiga,   se uuarot so ih ginigo.
So uuare sose ih cherte minen zoum,   so rado nami dus goum:
   den uuech furiuuorhtostu mir,   daz ih mih cherte after dir.
Du hapest mir de zungun   so fasto piduungen,
   daz ih ane din gipot   ne spricho nohein uuort.   10
Uuie michiliu ist   de din giuuizida, Christ,
   fone mir ce dir gitan!   Uuie mahtih dir intrinnen!
Far ih uf ze himile,   dar pistu mit herie,
   ist ze hello min fart,   dar pistu geginuuart:
   ne megih in nohhein lant,   nupe mih hapet din hant.   15
Nu uuillih mansleccun   alle fone mir gituon,
   alle die mir rieton   den unrehton rihtuom.
Alle die mir rietun   den unrehton rihtuom,
   die sint fienta din,   mit den uuillih gifeh sin.
De uuider dir uuellent tuon,   de uuillih fasto nidon,   20
   alle durh dinen ruom   mir ze fiente tuon.
Du got mit dinero giuualt   scirmi iogiuuedrehalp,
   mit dinero chrefti   pinim du mo daz scefti,
   ne la du mos de muozze,   daz er mih se ane skiozze.
De sela uuorhtostu mir,   die pisazi du mir.   25
   du uurti sar min giuuar,   so mih de muoter gipar.
Noh trof ih des ne lougino,   des du tati tougino,
   nupe ih fone gipurti   ze erdun auer uurti.

Psalm 138

Do you wish to hear   good king David speak clear,
   and the sense of his words?   Thus he spoke to the Lord:
Lord, you have found me   and know who I may be
   from my very birth   to the day of my death.
My thoughts in no way   could ever from you stray,
   All my paths you know   wherever I may go.
Where I may take my horse,   you soon know its course,
   and you direct my path too   so that I come to you.
My tongue you have bound   that I make not a sound,
   and without your bidding   cannot say a thing.
How great must it be,   Christ, your knowledge of me,
   so that I might   never flee from your sight.
If I should to heaven rise   you and your hosts are in the skies,
   if my path is to hell,   then you are there as well.
   I can go to no land   and not be in your hand.
Murderers shall be   cast away from me,
   all those who led me   to act wrongfully.
All those who led me   to act wrongfully
   are your enemies   and are mine likewise.
Those who act against you   I shall hate them too
   and for your honour's sake   foes of them I shall make.
O God, with your power   protect me every hour
   with the force of your word   take my enemies' sword
   so that he never might   attack me with spite.
You created my soul   and have possessed my soul
   watched carefully   since my mother bore me.
Nor can I deny   works not seen by the eye
   by which you keep me sure   from the dust I was born for.

Far ih in de finster,   dar hapest du mih sar:
   ih uueiz daz din nacht mach   sin so lioht also tach.   30
So uuillih danne file fruo   stellen mino federa:
   peginno ih danne fliogen   sose er ne tete nioman.
Peginno ih danne fliogen   sose er ne tete nioman,
   so fliugih ze enti ienes meres: ih uueiz daz du mih dar irferist;
   ne megih in nohhein lant,   nupe mih hapet din hant.   35
Nu chius dir fasto ze mir,   upe ih mih chere after dir:
   du ginadigo got,   cheri mih framort,
   mit dinen ginadun   gihalt mih dir in euun.

If into darkness I flee   you will still protect me,
    I know that even your night   is as bright as daylight.
So I shall soon begin   to spread open my wings,
    and begin to soar   as none has done before.
And begin to soar   as none has done before,
    to the ends of the sea,   and you still will see me,
    I can go to no land   and not be in your hand.
Now hold me in your clasp   as I to you grasp,
    most merciful one,   lead me ever on
    with your grace upon me   for eternity.

8

The Hymn to St Peter (*Petruslied*) and other Prayers

A few rhymed prayers and blessings survive in Old High German, of which the most interesting is the Hymn to St Peter, which survives in a manuscript with its musical notation (*neumes*). It is Bavarian, mid-ninth-century, has similarities with a Latin hymn to St Peter used for the feast day of Saints Peter and Paul on 29 June, and has the liturgical refrain *Kyrie eleison*, "Lord have mercy." Also Bavarian, from around 900, are Sigihart's prayers, which are found at the end of the Freising manuscript of Otfrid's Gospel-book, now in Munich. They are followed by the words *Uualdo epi[scopus] istud evangelium fieri iussit. Ego sigihardus indignus pr[es]b[y]t[er] scripsi* ("Bishop Waldo had this Gospel written. I, Sigihard the unworthy priest, wrote this"). Beside and above the prayers are the words *Tu autem domine mis[erere] nobis* ("O Lord have mercy upon us"). The late ninth-century Rhenish Franconian prayer from a manuscript originally from Augsburg and now in Munich adapts a prayer from the Litany of the Saints (*Deus qui proprium...*). The Weingarten *Reisesegen*, a blessing for a journey, might have been included amongst the charms, but it looks more like a prayer. This is a late text, from a twelfth-century manuscript (now in Stuttgart) from the abbey of Weingarten in Baden-Württemberg with psalms and other prayers. It has a striking amount of alliteration as well as rhyme.

90

The texts are Steinmeyer XXI, XX, XVIII, LXXVIII; MSD IX, XV, XIV, IV/8; Braune XXXIII, XXXVIII/2, XXXVII (Braune does not have the Weingarten text). Such secondary material as there is on these texts is mostly about the *Petruslied* (several with the music).

Gamber, Klaus. "Das altbairische Petruslied." In *Sacerdos et cantus Gregoriani magister: Festschrift Ferdinand Haberl*, edited by Franz A. Stein, 107–116. Regensburg: Bosse, 1977.

Hoffmann von Fallersleben, A. H. *Geschichte des deutschen Kirchenliedes* [1861]. Hildesheim: Olms, 1965, 8–29.

Müller-Blattau, Joseph. "Zu Form und Überlieferung der ältesten deutschen geistlichen Lieder." *Zeitschrift für Musikwissenschaft* 17 (1935): 129–148.

Stavenhagen, Lee. "Das 'Petruslied'." *Wirkendes Wort* 17 (1967): 21–28.

Petruslied

Unsar trohtin hat farsalt   sancte Petre giuualt,
  daz er mac ginerian   ze imo dingenten man.
    Kyrie eleyson,   Christe eleyson.
Er hapet ouh mit uuortun   himilriches portun:
  dar in mach er skerian   den er uuili nerian.   5
    Kirie eleison,   Christe eleyson.
Pittemes den gotes trut   alla samant upar lut,
  daz er uns firtanen   giuuerdo ginaden.
    Kirie eleyson,   Christe eleison.

Sigiharts Gebete

Du himilisco trohtin,   Ginade uns mit mahtin
  In din selbes riche,   Soso dir giliche.
Al[iter].
Trohtin Christ in himile,   Mit dines fater segane
  Ginade uns in euun,   Daz uuir niliden uueuuun.

Augsburger Gebet

Deus, cui proprium est misereri semper et parcere, suscipe depre-
cationem nostram, ut, quos catena delictorum constringit, miser-
atio tuae pietatis absoluat. Per [Iesum Christum dominum nos-
trum].

Got, thir eigenhaf ist,   thaz io genathih bist,
Intfaa gebet unsar   (thes bethurfun uuir sar),
thaz uns thio ketinun   bindent thero sundun,
thinero mildo,   genad intbinde haldo.

Weingartner Reisesegen

+ In nomine + patris + et filii + et spiritus + sancti +
Ic dir nach sihe,   Ic dir nach sendi
mit minin funf fingirin   funui undi funfzic engili.
Got mit gisundi   hein dich gisendi.

The Hymn to St Peter

Our Lord the power gave   to St Peter, to save
    and to free from all blame   those who call on his name.
        Kyrie eleison, Christe eleison.
By the word of the Lord   he is heaven's gate's ward;
    grant entry he can   if he would save a man.
        Kyrie eleison, Christe eleison.
To God's saint let us pray   and together all say:
    may he to sinful men   grant grace once again.
        Kyrie eleison, Christe eleison

Sigihart's Prayers

Heavenly Lord   grant us grace with your word
    to share your realm with you   if you wish us to.
Another
Christ, heaven's lord,   with the blessing of God
    grant us ever your will   that we suffer no ill.

Augsburg Prayer

*O God, whose nature is ever to show mercy and forbearance, receive
our petition: that the tender mercy of your piety may mildly absolve
us, whom the chains of sins bind. Through Jesus Christ our Lord.*

O God, whose property   is to show us mercy,
our prayers heed   in our great need,
that all men chained in   by the bonds of our sin
may receive in its place   the relief of your grace.

Weingarten Journey-Blessing

+ In the name of the + Father, and the + Son and the + Holy + Spirit +
As you go I see you   and send after you too
with these five fingers of mine   fifty-five angels divine,
so that God should send   you in health home again.

Offin si dir diz sigidor,   sami si dir diz seldidor.
Bislozin si dir diz wagidor,   sami si dir diz wafindor.

Des guotin sandi Ulrichis segen si vor dir vndi hindir dir vndi hobi dir vndi nebin dir gidan, swa du wonis vndi swa du sis, daz da alsi gut fridi si, alsi da weri, da min fravwi sandi Marie des heiligin Cristis ginas.

Pass through the gate of victory   and through the gate of amity,
Be closed to you the gate of uncertainty and closed the gate of weaponry.

May the blessing of good St Ulrich be before you and behind you
and over you and beside you wherever you are and wherever you
stay, that you shall enjoy such peace as there was when Our
Blessed Lady Mary bore Christ the most holy.

9

The Song of St George (*Georgslied*)

Where the *Hildebrandslied* is written in an impossibly mixed-up language and *Muspilli* is scrawled over a fine manuscript, the Alemannic *Georgslied*, composed perhaps around 900 and recorded in the Heidelberg manuscript of Otfrid, is highly problematic in a different way. The language seems thoroughly distorted—the word *spranc*, for example, appears as *psanr* and the letter *h* appears regularly after the vowel it is supposed to precede. Was it written by a dyslexic scribe? At all events, after it breaks off, the words *ihn nequeo Vuisolf* appear; the Latin *nequeo* means "I can't do it" and the first word may be German, *ih n[e]...* meaning the same thing: Wisolf the scribe apparently gave up. The text, therefore, has effectively to be deciphered and reassembled, and there have been different reconstructed versions (Braune prints two nineteenth-century versions, and see Haubrichs and Schützeichel). Many suggestions have been made, too, for the various gaps, such as that around line 48. There are repeated refrain-lines, either reiterating that George did these deeds, or that he rose again, which may indicate separate sections.

St George—Georgios of Cappadocia, here called Gorio—was a well-known saint, who in the legend performs several miracles, raises the dead, banishes a demon, and converts the Roman emperor's wife. However, he is also regularly killed and comes back to life and thus serves to an extent as a parallel to Christ. His adversary, a ruler here called Dacian, may be linked with the Roman emperor Galerius Valerius Maximianus, caesar—joint ruler— of the eastern empire under the anti-Christian emperor Diocletian, and emperor himself from 305–311. His family originated from Dacia, roughly modern-day Romania. His wife was not called Alexandria, however. George may have been killed in one of his persecutions in 303. Saint George's battle with the dragon, incidentally, does not become part of his legend until later in the Middle Ages.

This is the only saint's life in German that we have from this period. We may note, however, that a tenth-century German life of St Gall, supposed founder of the important monastery of St Gallen, was composed by Ratpert, but it survives now only in a Latin translation made perhaps a century later by Ekkehart IV, another monk of St Gallen, who died in 1060. This Latin text is in MSD XII, and there is a full treatment of it by Peter Osterwalder, *Das althochdeutsche Galluslied Ratperts und seine lateinischen Übersetzungen durch Ekkehart IV* (Berlin: de Gruyter 1982), with a text and a modern German translation. It makes for an interesting comparison with the life of St George, but we do not have a German text.

For better or worse, the text here follows Steinmeyer's version of the confused original (XIX; MSD XVII, Braune XXXV), and he also prints what the manuscript actually has. The sometimes short half-lines make finding even moderately plausible rhymes more difficult than usual, quite apart from the sense. Many of the secondary studies of the *Georgslied* are of course devoted to sorting out the text.

Haubrichs, Wolfgang. *Georgslied und Georgslegende im frühen Mittelalter*. Königsstein/T.: Scriptor, 1979.
Kolbe, P. R. "The Strophic Form of the *Georgslied.*" *MLN* 31 (1916): 19–23.

Schützeichel, Rudolf. *Codex Pal. Lat. 52*. Göttingen: Vandenhoek und Ruprecht: 1982.

Tschirch, Fritz. "Der heilige Georg als *figura Christi*." In *Festschrift Helmut de Boor*. Tübingen: Niemeyer, 1966, 1–19.

Georgslied

Georio fuor ze malo   mit mikilemo herigo,
  fone dero marko   mit mikilemo folko.
Fuor er ze demo ringe,   ze heuigemo dinge.
  daz thinc uuas marista,   kote liebosta.
Ferliez er uuereltrike,   keuuan er himilrike.   5
  daz keteta selbo   der mare crabo Georio.
Do sbuonen inen alla   kuninga so manega.
  uuolton si inen erkeren,   neuuolta ern es horen.
Herte uuas daz Georiger muot,   nehort er in es, segih guot,
  nub er al kefrumeti,   des er ce kote digeti.   10
  daz keteta selbo   sancte Gorio.
Do teilton si inen sare   ze demo karekare.
  dar met imo do fuoren   engila de skonen.
Dar fand er ceuuei uuib,   kenerit er daz ire lib:
  do uuorht er so skono   daz imbiz in frono.   15
  daz ceiken uuorhta dare   Georio ce uuare.
Georio do digita,   inan druhtin al geuuereta.
  inan druhtin al geuuereta,   des Gorio zimo digita.
Den tumben sprekenten,   den touben horenten,
  den plinten det er sehenten,   den halcen gangenten.   20
Ein sul stuont er manic iar,   uz spranc der loub sar.
  daz zeiken uuorhta dare   Gorio ze uuare.
Begont ez der rike man   file harte zurenan:
  Tacianus uuuoto   zurent ez uunterdrato.
Er quat, Gorio uuari   ein koukelari,   25
  hiez er Goriien fahen,   hiez en uzziehen,
  hiez en slahen harto   mit uunteruuasso suereto.
Daz uueiz ik, daz ist aleuuar,   uf erstuont sik Goriio dar,

The Song of St George

George rode to the assembly   with a great panoply,
   from his land   with a large band.
He rode to the place of judgement   for a thing of great moment,
   it was an important event   and Our Lord was content.
[George] renounced the world's might   for heaven's sight,
   All that was done   by the noble Count George alone.
Trying to persuade him   were many a king,
   wanting him to deny the Lord,   but he would not hear a word.
George's resolve was firm and true   not to listen, I assure you,
   and all things he did   that he had promised to God.
   All that was done   by Saint George alone.
He was soon condemned   and they imprisoned him.
   In prison with him were   many bright angels there.
Two women there he met   whose lives he saved yet,
   and gave them good food   with the help of the Lord.
   The miracle was truly done   by St George alone.
All things for which George prayed   the Lord to him gave.
   the Lord to him gave   that for which George to Him prayed.
He made the dumb speak clear   and he made the deaf hear,
   made the blind see,   and the lame walk freely.
On an ancient pillar of stone   leaves and branches were grown.
   That miracle was truly done   by St George alone.
The ruler, strong and rich   became enraged at this —
   the furious Dacian   was a very angry man.
He said that George   was a trickster and fraud,
   ordered him to be taken   and stripped naked.
   and quickly gave word   that he be killed by the sharpest sword,
I know it to be true that then   George rose up again.

uf erstuont sik Goriio dar,   wola predi[g]iot er dar.
  die heidenen man   kescante Gorio drate fram.   30
Begont ez der rike man   filo harto zurnan.
  do hiez er Goriion hinten,   anen rad uuinten:
  ce uuare sagen ik ez iu,   sie praken inen en ceniu.
Daz uueiz ik, daz ist aleuuar,   uf erstuont sik Gorio dar,
  uf erstuont sik Gorio dar,   uuola [. . .] dar.   35
  die heidenen man   kescante Gorio file fram.
Do hiez er Gorion fahen,   hiez en harto fillen.
  man gehiez en muillen,   ze puluer al uerprennen.
  man uuarf en in den prunnen: [...]
Poloton si der ubere   steine mikil menige.   40
  begonton si nen umbekan,   hiezen Gorien uf erstan.
  mikil teta Georio dar,   so er io tuot in war.
Daz uueiz ik, daz ist aleuuar,   uf erstuont sik Gorio dar,
  uf erstuont sik Gorio dar,   uz spranc der uuac sar.
  die heidenen man   kescante Gorio file fram.   45
Gorio einen toten man   uf hiez er stantan,
  er hiez en dare cimo kan,   hiez en sar sprekan.
Do segita [......]
  quuat, si uuarin florena,   demo tiufele al petrogena,
  daz cunt uns selbo   sancte Gorio.   50
Do gienc er ze dero kamero   ze dero chuninginno,
  pegont er sie leren,   begonta si mes horen.
Elossandria,   si uuas dogelika,
  si ilta sar uuole tuon,   den iro scaz spenton.
Si spentota iro triso dar: daz hilfet sa manec iar.   55
  fon euuon uncen euuon   so [...] en gnadon.
  daz erdigita selbo   hero sancte Gorio.
Gorio huob dia hant uf: erbibinota Abollin,
  gebot er uper den hellehunt: do fuor er sar en abcrunt.
ihn *nequeo Vuisolf*

George rose up again   and preached well there and then.
All the heathen men   George brought shame upon them.
Then the rich emperor   was angered all the more,
and had George bound,   tied on a wheel around.
I assure you   that they broke him in two
I know it to be true that then   George rose up again.
George rose up again   and [preached well] there and then.
All the heathen men,   George brought shame upon them.
The emperor gave word   that George should be scourged,
then that he be cut up   and then burnt to dust.
In a well he was cast...
They piled thereon   many great stones.
They circled about   and called on George to come out.
George did great things there   as he truly does everywhere.
I know it to be true that then   George rose up again.
George rose up again,   out sprang the most excellent man.
All the heathen men,   George brought shame upon them.
George commanded a dead man   to rise up again.
He told him to come near   and speak out clear,
He said ......
He said that they were lost to evil   and tricked by the devil.
This we know   since Saint George told us so.
George then went   to the queen's apartments,
gave her his teaching,   and she listened to him.
Alexandria   was of a virtue rare,
she hastened to do good   and gave as alms all she had.
Her gold and her gear,   gave aid for many a year.
now and evermore   she is in grace [with the Lord].
through the prayers and the word   of the worthy Saint George.
George raised his hand   and Apollyon was banned,
he conjured that hellhound with this   back into the abyss.
I cannot... *I cannot.* Wisolf

10

King Louis at Saucourt (*Ludwigslied*)

The background of the Old High German *Ludwigslied,* a 59-line rhymed poem in the Rhenish Franconian dialect, is as fortunate and as fortuitous as that of many of the other surviving texts. It celebrates the victory of King Louis III of the West Franks—of what is roughly modern France—over the Vikings at Saucourt in Picardy in August 881. Louis ruled from 879 until his death in August 882. The Carolingian dynasty used a limited set of regnal names, so that the post-Charlemagne kings of what is now Germany and France both alternated between Carolus and Ludovicus. To translate the latter uniformly as "Lewis" is a democratic solution, but using Louis and Ludwig at least distinguishes them. Louis III succeeded his father, Charlemagne's grandson Louis II, known as the Stammerer. He shared the throne with his brother, Carloman II, who continued to rule after 882, but he then died in 884. When Louis III was king of the West Franks, Germany (the East Franks) was ruled by Charles the Fat, son of Ludwig II, known as Ludwig the German. Louis III probably still spoke German (not, however, the same dialect as that of the poem), although the early stages of French was current in West Francia by then.

The poem's survival is also interesting. It is written on blank sheets of a Latin manuscript, beautifully laid out in strophic groups of two or three rhymed long lines, and it is very clear (in contrast, say, with *Muspilli* or the *Georgslied*). Together with it, however, is one of the earliest French poems (a saint's life), with a Latin poem on the same theme, and other Latin poetic material. These additions, and probably the manuscript itself, were written at the monastery of St Amand, near the present Belgian border and the manuscript is now in Valenciennes. It was first edited in the seventeenth century, but the manuscript was presumed to have been destroyed in a fire until it was re-discovered in the nineteenth (its interesting history is described by Lefrancq). Dating the poem's composition is for once an easy task. Louis is referred to as living, but he died a year after the battle described. It was presumably copied later, since the added Latin title makes it into a memorial piece. Apart from the language, however, the poem has absolutely no connection with what is now Germany. It is the only German text in a manuscript that has never left France. The theme, too, is West Frankish—the victory of a West Frankish king on West Frank soil. In German one might have expected a poem celebrating the deeds of Ludwig the German. What seems likely is that it was composed by a monk at St Amand, originally from the Rhineland, but of course a subject of King Louis III.

The subject is historical. Vikings (North-men, Norsemen) attacked France and the Low Countries after their defeat in 878 in England by King Alfred (they eventually settled in the area which still has their name, Normandy). Louis had been with his brother Carloman defending their southern lands, but he returned north and engaged with the Vikings unexpectedly on 3 August 881, defeating them. The poet's approach to history, however, is theocentric: the whole incident is divinely planned. The Vikings, who are not especially vilified, are portrayed as a scourge sent by God to punish the sins of the people and to test the young king. The Franks' battle song is the *Kyrie eleison* ("Lord have mercy"). God speaks directly to Louis, who does what he is instructed and fights bravely. God is outside historical time, but even kings do not know how events will work out, and must simply act according to their duty. At the end there is a sharp distinction, underscored by the paratactic style, between the thanks given to God and Louis's victory as such.

The text is in Steinmeyer XVI, MSD XI, Braune XXXVI. There is a small gap at line 57, where I accept the reading *wigsalig* (glorious in victory) but other suggestions have been made. The rhymes are often imperfect by modern standards. Much of the secondary literature is concerned with the presentation of history and with the theology of the work.

Berg, Elisabeth. "Das *Ludwigslied* und die Schlacht bei Saucourt." *Rheinische Vierteljahrsblätter* 29 (1964): 175–199.

Händl, Claudia. *Ludwigslied. Canto di Ludovico. Introduzione e commento*. Alessandria: Edizioni dell'Orso, 1990.

Harvey, Ruth. "The Provenance of the Old High German *Ludwigslied*." *Medium Aevum* 14 (1945): 1–20.

Herweg, Mathias. *Ludwigslied, De Heinrico, Annolied*. Wiesbaden: Reichert, 2002.

Fouracre, Paul. "The Context of the OHG 'Ludwigslied'." *Medium Aevum* 54 (1985): 87–103.

Fouracre, Paul. "Using the Background to the *Ludwigslied*. Some Methodological Problems." In *Mit regulu bithuungan. Neue Arbeiten zur althochdeutschen Poesie und Sprache*, edited by John L. Flood and David N. Yeandle, 80–93. Göppingen: Kümmerle, 1989.

Lefrancq, Paul. *"Rhythmus Teutonicus" ou "Ludwigslied."* Paris: Droz, 1945.

Maurer, Friedrich. "Hildebrandslied und Ludwigslied." *Der Deutschunterricht* 9/2 (1957): 5–15.

Murdoch, Brian. "Saucourt and the *Ludwigslied*." *Revue belge d'histoire et de philologie* 55 (1977): 841–867.

Schwarz, Werner. "The 'Ludwigslied', a Ninth Century Poem." *Modern Language Review* 42 (1947): 467–473.

Urmoneit, Erika. *Der Wortschatz des Ludwigsliedes im Umkreis der althochdeutschen Literatur*. Munich: Fink, 1973.

Willems, Fritz. "Der parataktische Satzstil im *Ludwigslied*," *Zeitschrift für deutsches Altertum* 85 (1954/5): 18–35.

Yeandle, David. "The *Ludwigslied*: King, Church, and Context." In *Mit regulu bithuungan. Neue Arbeiten zur althochdeutschen Poesie und Sprache,* edited by John L. Flood and David N. Yeandle, 18–79. Göppingen: Kümmerle, 1989.

Ludwigslied

Rithmus teutonicus de piae memoriae Hluduico rege filio Hluduici aeque regis.

Einan kuning uueiz ih,   Heizsit her Hluduig,
  Ther gerno gode thionot: Ih uueiz her imos lonot.
Kind uuarth her faterlos.   Thes uuarth imo sar buoz:
  Holoda inan truhtin.   Magaczogo uuarth her sin.
Gab her imo dugidi,   Fronisc githigini,   5
  Stuol hier in Urankon.   So bruche her es lango!
Thaz gideilder thanne   Sar mit Karlemanne,
  Bruoder sinemo,   Thia czala uuunniono.
So thaz uuarth al gendiot,   Koron uuolda sin god,
  Ob her arbeidi   So iung tholon mahti.   10
Lietz her heidine man   Obar seo lidan,
  Thiot Urancono   Manon sundiono.
Sume sar uerlorane   Uuurdun sum erkorane.
  Haranskara tholota   Ther er misselebeta.
Ther ther thanne thiob uuas,   Inder thanana ginas,   15
  Nam sina uaston: Sidh uuarth her guot man.
Sum uuas luginari,   Sum skachari,
  Sum fol loses,   Inder gibuozta sih thes.
Kuning uuas eruirrit,   Thaz richi al girrit,
  Uuas erbolgan Krist: Leidhor, thes ingald iz.   20
Thoh erbarmedes got,   Uuisser alla thia not:
  Hiez her Hluduigan   Tharot sar ritan.
"Hluduig, kuning min,   Hilph minan liutin!
  Heigun sa Northman   Harto biduuungan."
Thanne sprah Hluduig: "Herro, so duon ih,   25
  Dot nirette mir iz,   Al thaz thu gibiudist".

King Louis at Saucourt

A German poem in blessed memory of King Louis, the son of Louis,
who was also king.

A king is known to me, named Sir Louis,
 who gladly served Our Lord. I know he gained his reward.
Fatherless as a young man, help was yet at hand,
 the Lord God took him in and acted as his kin.
He gave him every virtue and strong companions, too,
 a throne with the Franks here. May he hold it for years!
He shared it all then with Carloman,
 with his brother–king all these wonderful things.
When that was all settled God wished to try his mettle,
 if he could withstand hardship as such a young man.
God sent the pagans across the sea to his land,
 so the Franks might pay for their sinful ways.
Some went to their graves, some of them were saved,
 there was great suffering on those mired in sin.
If one had been a thief and was granted relief,
 afterwards he would fast, and be a good man at last.
Some had lied to excess, some had done wickedness,
 some had been lustful men, but they did penance then.
The king was far away, his land is disarray.
 Christ's angry hand was felt by the land.
But God relented again. He knows all our pain!
 He told Louis at once to ride back to France.
"Louis, my king, help my folk's suffering.
 The Norsemen have come and inflicted great harm."
Said King Louis, "this task I shall take as you ask,
 if I am not killed, I shall do all your will."

Tho nam her godes urlub,   Huob her gundfanon uf,
  Reit her thara in Urankon   Ingagan Northmannon.
Gode thancodun   The sin beidodun,
  Quadhun al: "fro min,   So lango beidon uuir thin".   30
Thanne sprah luto   Hluduig ther guoto:
  "Trostet hiu, gisellion,   Mine notstallon.
Hera santa mih god   Ioh mir selbo gibod,
  Ob hiu rat thuhti,   Thaz ih hier geuuhti,
  Mih selbon ni sparoti,   Uncih hiu gineriti.   35
Nu uuillih, thaz mir uolgon   Alle godes holdon.
  Giskerit ist thiu hieruuist   So lango so uuili Krist;
  Uuili her unsa hinauarth,   Thero habet her giuualt.
So uuer so hier in ellian   Giduot godes uuillion,
  Quimit he gisund uz,   Ih gilonon imoz;   40
  Bilibit her thar inne,   Sinemo kunnie."
Tho nam her skild indi sper,   Ellianlicho reit her:
  Uuolder uuar errahchon   Sinan uuidarsahchon.
Tho ni uuas iz burolang,   Fand her thia Northman:
  Gode lob sageda,   Her sihit thes her gereda.   45
Ther kuning reit kuono,   Sang lioth frano,
  Ioh alle saman sungun   "Kyrrieleison".
Sang uuas gisungan,   Uuig uuas bigunnan,
  Bluot skein in uuangon: Spilodun ther Urankon.
Thar uaht thegeno gelih,   Nichein soso Hluduig: 50
  Snel indi kuoni,   Thaz uuas inio gekunni.
Suman thuruhskluog her,   Suman thuruhstah her.
  Her skancta ce hanton   Sinan fianton
  Bitteres lides.   So uue hin hio thes libes!
Gilobot si thiu godes kraft!   Hluduig uuarth sigihaft.   55
  Ioh allen heiligon thanc!   Sin uuarth ther sigikamf.
Uuolar abur Hluduig,   Kuning [uuig]salig!
  So garo soser hio uuas,   So uuar soses thurft uuas,
  Gihalde inan truhtin   Bi sinan ergrehtin!

From God he withdrew,   then the war-banners flew,
    and homeward he rode   to fight the Norse horde.
They gave God thank-offerings   those who awaited the king,
    and said: "Sire, it is true   we have waited long for you."
Then spoke loudly   the noble King Louis:
    "Have no more care,   my brothers in war.
God sent me to our land   and gave me His command,
    that if you think it is right,   that I should fight
    and not rest from toil   until I have saved you all.
I want with me here   all who hold God dear.
    Our time here below   is what Christ will allow,
    and if He wants our end,   that is His to command.
Any man who fights with skill,   does the Lord's will,
    and if he should survive,   rewards to him I'll give,
    or if he should die,   then to his family."
He took up shield and spear   and rode boldly from there,
    To take a strong message to   the opposing foe.
It did not take long   to meet with the Norse throng,
    he praised God aloud!   Those he sought had been found.
Fiercely the king rode,   and a hymn he intoned,
    and all of them that day   sang out "Kyrie."
The song had been sung,   the battle begun,
    blood made each face shine,   in the Franks' joyful line.
There no man fought as fiercely   as did King Louis,
    swift and bold,   that was bred in his blood.
Some he struck through,   some he ran through,
    he served right away   to his enemies that day
    a most bitter beer.   Their lives were put in fear!
Let God's powers praised be!   Louis had the victory.
    And thank the saints we must!   Louis was victorious.
All glory to Louis,   a king blessed with victory,
    always ready indeed   to be there when there was need.
    May the Lord keep his place   in His holy grace.

11

De Heinrico

The other historical poem in Old High German—or in this case at least partly so, since it is a mixture of Latin and German—is found in the celebrated collection of poems known because of its present location as the *Cambridge Songs,* an eleventh-century manuscript written probably in Canterbury, in England, although the original was certainly German. The manuscript has various Latin poems on patently German themes (Müllenhoff and Scherer included several in their collection), as well as two macaronic pieces. One is the very fragmentary piece known as *Suavissima nonna (Kleriker und Nonne),* but it is not included in this anthology because so little of it remains, even though it has been valiantly reconstructed by Peter Dronke (*Medieval Latin and the Rise of European Love Lyric*, Oxford: Clarendon 1966, II, 353–6, with a translation). The other piece, however, *De Heinrico,* is a poem of long lines arranged in strophes (three with four lines, five with three) about a certain Duke Heinrich/Henry of Bavaria. The poem is macaronic, with the first half of each long line usually in Latin, the second half in German, but with occasional mix-ups, some of which (as in the slightly disordered first line) can be corrected. The dialect is Rhenish Franconian, though it may have been adapted from a different original. It looks rather like a kind of intellectual exercise, which is possibly always the case with macaronic texts. There are some linguistic or interpretative problems; there are Low German elements, and there is a baffling reference to "two of the same name" in strophe 4.

The precise historical background is not clear. The duke, who arrives with a body of men, is welcomed by Emperor Otto, and they go to mass. This may refer to Otto I (936–973) and his rebellious younger brother Henry, later Duke of Bavaria; or to Otto III (983–1002) and Henry the Quarrelsome, Duke Henry II of Bavaria, who was equally rebellious, but was also eventually reinstated in his duchy. Whichever duke is involved, he is received with great honour and becomes a trusty and in fact prominent advisor who does not—we are assured very firmly—want the crown himself. It may have been written during the reign of Emperor Henry II (1014–24), grandson of the first rebellious Duke of Bavaria and son of the second, to make either or both look more respectable.

The text is from Steinmeyer XXIII with some emendation from Braune XXXIX. It is MSD XVIII. This work presents a problem in a collection the aim of which is to try to give a fairly close approximation of the original in English. Accordingly, an attempt has been made to rhyme with the Latin (assuming ecclesiastical pronunciation and noting again that the rhymes are not always very close). For general comprehension, however, a crib version is appended with the Latin sections translated. The historical background has been much discussed, most extensively by Herweg.

Dittrich, Marie Luise. "De Heinrico." *Zeitschrift für deutsches Altertum* 84 (1952/3): 274–308.

Herweg, Mathias. *Ludwigslied, De Heinrico, Annolied.* Wiesbaden: Reichert, 2002.

Jungandreas, Wolfgang. "De Heinrico." *Leuvense Bijdragen* 57 (1968): 75–91.

Ochs, Ernst. "*Ambo vos aequivoci.* Zur Abfassungszeit des ahd-
   lat. Heinrichslied." *Zeitschrift für deutsche Philologie* 66 (1941):
   10–12.
Uhlirz, Mathilde. "Der Modus 'De Heinrico' und sein geschicht-
   licher Inhalt." *Deutsche Vierteljahresschrift* 26 (1952): 153–
   161.

De Heinrico

1. Nunc almus [assis filius   thero euuigun thiernun]
        benignus fautor mihi,   thaz ig iz cosan muozi
        de quodam duce,   themo heron Heinriche,
        qui cum dignitate   thero Beiaro riche beuuarode.

2. Intrans nempe nuntius   then keisar namoda her thus   5
        "cur sedes?" infit, "Otdo,   ther unsar keisar guodo.
        hic adest Heinrich,   bringit her hera kuniglich.
        dignum tibi fore   thir seluemo ze sine."

3. Tunc surrexit Otdo,   ther unsar keisar guodo,
        perrexit illi obuiam   inde uilo manig man   10
        et excepit illum   mid mihilon eron.

4. Primitus quoque dixit: "uuillicumo Heinrich.
        ambo uos equiuoci,   bethiu goda endi mi,
        nec non et sotii,   uuillicumo sid gi mi".

5. Dato responso   fane Heinriche so scono   15
        coniunxere manus;   her leida ina in thaz godes hus:
        petierunt ambo   thero godes genatheno.

6. Oramine facto   intfieg ina auer Otdo,
        duxit in concilium   mit michelon eron
        et omisit illi   so uuaz so her thar hafode,   20
        preter quod regale,   thes thir Heinrih nigerade.

On Duke Heinrich

1. Nunc almus assis filius   of the eternal virgin glorious
    benignus fautor mihi,   that I may tell the history
    de quodam duce,   named Lord Heinrich,
    qui cum dignitate   ruled Bavaria's country.

2. Intrans nempe nuntius   and addressed the emperor thus:
    "cur sedes?" infit, "Otdo,   our good emperor, I wish to know;
    hic adest Heinrich,   bringing a royal entourage,
    dignum tibi fore   to be yours surely."

3. Tunc surrexit Otdo,   our good emperor now,
    perrexit illi obuiam   with a great body of men
    et excepit illum   in honourable fashion.

4. Primitus quoque dixit: "You are welcome, Heinrich.
    ambo uos equiuoci,   both to God and to me,
    nec non et sotii,   let them all welcome be."

5. Dato responso   by Heinrich nobly,
    coniunxere manus;   he led him into God's house:
    petierunt ambo   for God's grace here below.

6. Oramine facto   he was received by Otto,
    duxit in concilium   with honour and acclaim
    et omisit illi   every dignity,
    preter quod regale,   which Heinrich desired in no way.

7. Tunc stetit al thiu sprakha   sub firmo Heinriche.
     quicquid Otdo fecit,   al geried iz Heinrih;
     quicquid ac omisit,   ouch geried iz Heinrihe.

8. Hic non fuit ullus   (thes hafon ig guoda fulleist   25
     nobilibus ac liberis,   thaz thid allaz uuar is)
     cui non fecisset Heinrich   allero rehto gilich.

7. Tunc stetit all decisions reached   sub firmo of Heinrich.
    quicquid Otdo fecit,   was advised by Heinrich;
    quicquid ac omisit,   Heinrich advised him upon it.

8. Hic non fuit ullus   (I have reliable witness
    nobilibus ac liberis,   of the truth of all this)
    cui non fecisset Heinrich   all of their rights to each.

A Key to the Latin:

1. *Now may the noble son*   of the eternal virgin glorious
my kindly patron, help me,   that I may tell the history
of a certain duke,   named Lord Heinrich,
who with dignity   ruled Bavaria's country.

2. *Once an envoy came in*   and addressed the emperor thus:
"Why are you seated" he said, "Otto,   our good emperor, I wish to know?
Here is Heinrich,   bringing a royal entourage,
Worthy of you,   to be yours surely."

3. *So Otto arose,*   our good emperor now,
and went to meet him then   with a great body of men
and received him   in honourable fashion.

4. *He spoke first:*   "You are welcome, Heinrich.
You two of the same name,   both to God and to me,
not forgetting your companions,   let them all welcome be."

5. *A reply having been given*   by Heinrich nobly,
they joined hands;   he led him into God's house:
both men prayed   for God's grace here below.

6. *After the prayer*   he was received by Otto,
and led into the council   with honour and acclaim,
and afforded him   every dignity,
except the crown,   which Heinrich did not desire anyway.

7. *Then were* all decisions reached   *subject to* Heinrich.
Whatever Otto did,   was advised by Heinrich;
whatever he left undone,   Heinrich advised him upon it.

8. *There was not a single person*   (I have reliable witness
from nobles and freemen   of the truth of all this)
to whom Heinrich did not grant   all their rights to each.

12

Minor Texts

The last few fragments are something of a mixed bag, and their dates and meanings are not always at all clear. The Middle Franconian inscription from Cologne (possible late ninth century) is known only from a sixteenth century engraving, where it was part of a decoration—it seems to have been placed over a library door. There are further little pieces (tenth–eleventh century, Alemannic) written into theological and even biblical manuscripts in St Gallen. One is a scribe's comment, and another consists of two apparently satirical verses, in the second of which the name "Starzfidere" may well be somewhat improper, though it could just mean "shorty." Also originally from St Gallen (the manuscript is now in Brussels) is *Hirsch und Hinde*, "Hart and Hind," which has attracted much attention, for all that we only have nine words of it. Ute Schwab's extensive study establishes that is not just a line used by a scribe to test his pen, but what it actually is—an early love-song?—will remain enigmatic. Finally, the prolific scholar, writer, and translator Notker III (Labeo, the German) of St Gallen, who died in 1022, did a great deal to establish a tradition of German prose, and in his work on rhetoric he included as examples of rhetorical flourishes such as hyperbole two (or possibly three, if the last three lines are separate) little German verses, which have again attracted much attention.

Some of the texts are in Steinmeyer LXXXII, LXXXIII, LXXIX; MSD XXVIII, XV, VI; the Notker-verses are in Braune (XL). The Cologne inscription is in Gerhard Köbler, *Sammlung kleinerer althochdeutscher Sprachdenkmäler* (Giessen: Arbeiten zur Rechts- und Sprachwissenschaft Verlag, 1986), p. 238f. The secondary studies—especially the earlier ones—are often speculative and sometimes interestingly inventive.

Beck, Heinrich. *Das Ebersignum im Germanischen.* Berlin: de Gruyter, 1965.

Bergmann, Rolf. "Zu der althochdeutschen Inschrift aus Köln." *Rheinische Vierteljahrsblätter* 30 (1965): 66–69 (with an illustration).

Edwards, Cyril. "*winileodos*? Zu Nonnen, Zensur und den Spuren des althochdeutschen Liebeslyrik." In *Theodisca*, edited by Wolfgang Haubrichs et al., 189–206. Berlin and New York: de Gruyter, 2000 (on *Hirsch und Hinde*).

Frings, Theodor. "Hirsch und Hinde." *Beiträge zur Geschichte der deutschen Sprache und Literatur*/Halle 85 (1963): 22–26.

Henning, R. "Kleine Mitteilungen. *Starzfidere.*" *Zeitschrift für deutsches Altertum* 30 (1908–1909): 111f.

Kip, H. Z. "Ein unverstandener ahd. Spottvers." *MLN* 23 (1908): 106–108. (on the first satirical verse).

Schädel, B. "Der heber gat in litun." *Zeitschrift für deutsche Philologie* 9 (1878): 93–99.

Naumann, Hans. "Der große Eber." *Beiträge zur Geschichte der deutschen Sprache und Literatur* 45 (1921): 473–477.

Schwab, Ute. "Eber, aper und porcus in Notkers des Deutschen 'Rhetorik'", *Annali dell'Istituto Orientale di Napoli*/Sez. Ling. 8 (1967): 1–137.

Schwab, Ute. "Das althochdeutsche Lied 'Hirsch und Hinde' in seiner lateinischen Umgebung." In *Latein und Volkssprache im deutschen Mittelalter 1100-1500*, edited by Nikolaus Henkel and Nigel F. Palmer, 74–122. Tübingen: Niemeyer, 1992.

Schwab, Ute. "'Hirez runeta' und die lateinischen Randeinträge im Cod. Brux. 8860-8867. 'Hirsch und Hinde und die Otmar Antiphonen'" (1993). In *Weniger wäre. Ausgewählte kleine Schriften*, edited by Ute Schwab, 413–467. Vienna: Fassbaender, 2003.

Kölner Inschrift

hir maht thu lernan guld beuueruan,
uuelog inde uui[s]duom sigi[nuft inde ruom].

Schreibervers (St Gallen)

Chumo kiscreib, filo chumor kipeit.

Spottverse (St Gallen)

1
churo comsic herenlant aller oter lestilant.

2
Liubene ersazta sine gruz unde kab sina tohter uz:
to cham aber Starzfidere, prahta imo sina tohter uuidere.

Hirsch und Hinde

Hirez runeta hintun in daz ora:
"uuildu noh, hinta, ...?"

Aus Notkers "Rhetorik"

1
Sose snel snellemo pegagenet andermo,
so uuirdet sliemo firsniten sciltriemo.

2
Der heber gat in litun, tregit sper in situn:
sin bald ellin ne lazet in vellin.
Imo sint fuoze fuodermaze,
imo sint burste ebenho forste
unde zene sine zuuelifelnige.

Cologne Inscription

Here you may learn,   gold to earn,
Wealth and wisdom to gain,   victory and fame.

Scribe's Verse from St Gallen

I struggled to write this verse,   and how long it took me was
even worse.

Satirical Verses from St Gallen

1
The foreigner came to this land   and only this one he found grand.

2
Liubene served up the beer today   and gave his daughter away;
But then Featherbutt came   and brought his daughter back again.

Hart and Hind

The hart whispered clear   words into the hind's ear
"Will you, dear hind…"

Verses from Notker's *Rhetoric*

1
If a warrior should meet   another just as fleet,
then without ado,   shieldstraps will be hacked in two.

2
The boar goes on the hill-track   with a spear in its back,
but his strength abounds,   does not let him fall down.
His feet   are massive and great,
his bristles as tall   as a forest wall,
and his tusks are strong   and twelve yards long.

Appendix

Old Low German (Old Saxon) Parallels

I.   Charms

1

(Steinmeyer LXVII/A. A parallel to the charm *Pro Nessia)*

Contra vermes
Gang ut, nesso,   mid nigun nessiklinon,
ut fana themo marge an that ben,   fan themo bene an that flesg,
ut fan themo flesge an thia hud,   ut fan thera hud an thesa strala.
    drohtin, uuerthe so!

2

(Steinmeyer LXV. A horse-charm from the same theological ma-
nuscript)

De hoc quod spvrihalz dicvnt.
Primvm pater noster
Visc flot aftar themo uuatare,   uerbrustun sina uetherun.
tho gihelida ina use druhtin.

the seluo druhtin, thie thena uisc gihelda, thie gihele that hers
theru spurihelti.
Amen.

1

Against disease-worms
Begone, worm   with nine wee wormlets,
out of the marrow into the bone   out of the bone into the flesh
out of the flesh into the skin   out of the skin into this arrow.
    Lord, let it be!

2

Of that which is called lameness.
First one Paternoster
Fish swam in the flood   fractured its fins.
Then Our Lord healed it.

May the Lord himself, who healed the fish, heal this horse of
lameness.
Amen

II. The *Heliand*

Heliand, ed. Eduard Sievers (Halle/S.: Waisenhaus, 1878); *Heliand und Genesis*, ed. Otto Behaghel, 10th ed. by Burkhard Taeger (Tübingen: Niemeyer, 1996).

1
VIII, vv. 630–699 (The Magi)

<pre>
Tho gifragn ic that san aftar thiu   sliðmod cuning   630
thero uuarsagono uuord   them uurekkiun sagda,
thea thar an elilendi   erlos uuarun
ferran gifarana,   endi he fragoda aftar thiu,
huan sie an ostaruuegun   erist gisahin
thana cuningsterron cuman,   cumbal liuhtien   635
hedro fon himile.   Sie ni uueldun is im tho helen eouuiht,
ac sagdun it im soðlico.   Tho het he sie an thana sið faran,
het that sie ira arundi   al undarfundin
umbi thes kindes cumi,   endi the cuning selƀo gibod
suiðo hardlico,   herro Iudeono,   640
them uuisun mannun,   er than sie forin uuestan forð,
that sie im eft gicuðdin,   huar he thana cuning scoldi
sokean at is selðon;   quað that he thar uueldi mid is gisiðun to,
bedan te them barne.   Than hogda he im te banon uuerðan
uuapnes eggiun.   Than eft uualdand god   645
thahte uuið them thinga: he mahta athengean mer,
gilestean an thesum liohte: that is noh lango skin,
gicuðid craft godes.   Tho gengun eft thiu cumbal forð
uuanum undar uuolcnun.   Tho uuarun thea uuison man
fusa te faranne: giuuitun im forð thanan   650
balda an bodskepi: uueldun that barn godes
selƀon sokean.   Sie ni habdun thanan gisiðeas mer,
</pre>

1

The Magi

I heard that when   the wicked king
gave the prophets' words   to the wanderers,
who in their homeland   were honoured men
and had travelled far,   that he told them to tell him
when they fared from the east   they first saw
the king's star coming,   the clear-shining sign,
bright in the heavens.   They hid nothing from him,
and told him truth.   He urged the travellers
their task to fulfil,   to find out
about the coming of the child;   the king ordered
them loud and clear,   the lord of the Jews,
that these wise men   before they went westwards
should come and tell him   where he this king could
seek out himself,   saying he and his men would
this child worship.   He wanted to kill him,
with a sword's edge.   But Eternal God
had thought about this: there was more for him to do,
and his light   longer should shine
and God's power show.   Then the sign moved on,
shining through white clouds.   The wise men wished
to go further;   forth they went,
on with their search   for the son of God,
and him they sought.   No servants were with them,

butan that sie thrie uuarun: uuissun im thingo gisked,
uuarun im glauue gumon,   the thea geƀa leddun.
Than sahun sie so uuislico   undar thana uuolcnes skion,   655
up te them hohon himile,   huo forun thea huuiton sterron
—antkendun sie that cumbal godes—,   thiu uuarun thurh Krista herod
giuuarht te thesero uueroldi.   Thea uueros aftar gengun,
folgodun ferahtlico   — sie frumide the mahte —
antthat sie gisahun,   siðuuorige man,   660
berht bocan godes,   blec an himile
stillo gistanden.   The sterro liohto sken
huuit oƀar them huse   thar that helage barn
uuonode an uuilleon   endi ina that uuif biheld,
thiu thiorne githiudo.   Tho uuarð thero thegno hugi   665
bliði an iro briostun: bi them bocna forstodun,
that sie that friðubarn godes   funden habdun,
helagna heƀencuning.   Tho sie an that hus innan
mid iro gebun gengun,   gumon ostronea,
siðuuorige man: san antkendun   670
thea uueros uualdand Krist.   Thea uurekkion fellun
te them kinde an kneobeda   endi ina an cuninguuisa
godan grottun   endi im thea geƀa drogun,
gold endi uuihroc   bi godes tecnun
endi myrra thar mid.   Thea man stodun garouua,   675
holde for iro herron,   thea it mid iro handun san
fagaro antfengun.   Tho giuuitun im thea ferahton man,
seggi te selðon   siðuuorige,
gumon an gastseli.   Thar im godes engil
slapandiun an naht   suueƀan gitogde,   680
gidrog im an drome,   al so it drohtin self,
uualdand uuelde, that im thuhte that man im mid uuordun gibudi
that sie im thanan oðran uueg,   erlos forin,
liðodin sie te lande   endi thana leðan man,
Erodesan   eft ni sohtin,   685
modagna cuning.   Tho uuarð morgan cuman
uuanum te thesero uueroldi.   Tho bigunnun thea uuison man

they were just three;   all things they understood,
these men were clever   and came bearing gifts.
Knowingly they gazed   through the grey clouds
far into the sky   where the stars run bright
— seeing God's sign —   stars set by Christ,
made for this world.   They went after it,
followed in faith   — God's force helped them —
till they were aware,   these weary wanderers,
of God's bright sign   shining in the sky,
now staying still.   The starlight shone
bright over the house   where the holy child
lived willingly,   and the woman held him,
the virgin most dear.   The minds of the men
became blithe;   by the bright sign they knew
that they pursued   the peace-bringing Son of God,
the holy king of heaven.   The house they entered,
with their gifts,   these great men from the East,
weary from the road: they recognised him,
Christ, lord of the world.   The wanderers fell
and knelt by the babe   as befits a king,
greeted him grandly,   and gave gifts,
frankincense and gold,   the Godhead indicating,
and also myrrh.   The men stood ready,
respecting their ruler,   receiving him in their hands
in the best way.   The weary men then
wanted to rest,   road-weary as they were,
in the guesthouse.   God's angel there,
as at night they slept,   sent them a dream,
letting them know   what the Lord himself,
the Almighty, desired;   they dreamt they were told
that by a different road   return they must
to their own land,   and with the loathsome man,
Herod himself,   have no dealing,
the angry king.   Came the morning,
fine in the world,   the wise men

seggean iro sueƀanos: selƀon antkendun
uualdandes uuord,   huuand sie giuuit mikil
barun an iro briostun: badun alouualdon,   690
heron heƀencuning,   that sie mostin is huldi forð
giuuirkean is uuilleon,   quaðun that sea ti im habdin giuuendit hugi,
iro mod morgan gihuuem.   Tho forun eft thie man thanan,
erlos ostronie,   al so im the engil godes
uuordun giuuisde: namun im uueg oðran,   695
fulgengun godes lerun: ni uueldun them Iudeono cuninge
umbi thes barnes giburd   bodon ostronie,
siðuuorige man   seggian giouuiht,
ac uuendun   im eft an iro uuillion.

recounted their dream,   and recognised
the Lord's words —   wisdom they had,
deep in their breasts.   They begged the Almighty,
great heaven's lord,   that in grace they should walk
in accord with His will,   said they wished in their hearts
for that every new morning.   The Magi then made their way,
these wise men from the east,   as the angel of God
had to them declared,   by a different road.
As God commanded,   to the King of the Jews
about the child's birth the Magi,   the men from the east,
the weary wanderers   not a word would say,
but they went   their own way.

2

XIX, vv. 1600–1612 (The Lord's Prayer)

Pater noster: Fadar usa   firiho barno,   1600
thu bist an them hohon   himila rikea,
geuuihid si thin namo   uuordo gehuuilico.
Cuma thin   craftag riki.
Uuerða thin uuilleo   oƀar thesa uuerold alla,
so sama an erðo,   so thar uppa ist   1605
an them hohon   himilo rikea.
Gef us dago gehuuilikes rad,   drohtin the godo,
thina helaga helpa.   Endi alat us, heƀenes uuard,
managoro mensculdio,   al so uue oðrum mannum doan.
Ne lat us farledean   leða uuihti   1610
so forð an iro uuilleon,   so uui uuirðige sind,
ac help us uuiðar allun   uƀilon dadiun.

2

The Lord's Prayer

Paternoster. Our father   for all men,
you are in the high   heavenly kingdom,
may your name be sanctified   with all that we say.
May there come   your kingdom of greatness.
Your will be done   over the world,
the same on earth   as above
in the high   heavenly kingdom.
Give us each day your aid,   almighty lord,
your holy help.   Heaven's keeper, forgive us
our many misdeeds   as we other men forgive.
Let us not be led   by loathsome demons
to do their will,   but if we are worthy,
help us strive against   all evil deeds.

Bibliography

I. *Texts*

Note: Those marked with an asterisk include modern German translations. Editions of Otfrid's *Evangelienbuch* are listed in the introduction to chapter 5, but some of the collections include extracts from this work. English translations of some of the texts may be found in secondary studies or are available on the internet, principally the *Hildebrandslied*, which is in Bruce Dickens, *Runic and Heroic Poems of the Old Teutonic Peoples* (Cambridge: Cambridge University Press, 1915); there are more pieces (including the *Ludwigslied*) translated a century later by Philip Wilson, *The Bright Rose: Early German Verse 800-1280* (Todmorden: Arc, 2015). Recordings have been made of readings of some of the texts, most notably Otfrid. For facsimiles of Old High German manuscripts, see Eis and Fischer; most of the entries in the collective volume edited by Hasty and Hardin also have images of the relevant manuscripts, as do many individual studies.

Barber, Charles Clyde. *An Old High German Reader*. Oxford: Blackwell, 1951.

Burkhard, Werner. *Kleines althochdeutsches Lesebuch*, 2nd ed. Berne: Francke, 1946.

Braune, Wilhelm. *Althochdeutsches Lesebuch*, cont. by Karl Helm, 17th ed. by Ernst Ebbinghaus. Tubingen: Niemeyer, 1994.

Eis, Gerhard. *Altdeutsche Handschriften*. Munich: Beck, 1949.

Fischer, Hanns. *Schrifttafeln zum althochdeutschen Lesebuch*. Tubingen: Niemeyer, 1966.

Kienast, Richard. *Ausgewählte althochdeutsche Sprachdenkmäler*. Heidelberg: Winter, 1948.

Köbler, Gerhard. *Sammlung kleinerer althochdeutscher Sprachdenkmäler*. Giessen: Arbeiten zur Rechts- und Sprachwissenschaft Verlag, 1986.

Leyen, Friedrich von der. *Älteste deutsche Dichtungen*. Frankfurt/M.: Insel, 1964*.

Lösel, Franz. *A Short Old High German Grammar and Reader*. Dublin: Dublin University Press, 1969.

Mansion, Joseph. *Althochdeutsches Lesebuch*, 2nd ed. Heidelberg: Winter, 1932.

Mettke, Heinz. *Altdeustche Texte*. Leipig: Bibliographisches Institut, 1970.

Mettke, Heinz. *Älteste deutsche Dichtung und Prosa*. Leipzig: Reclam, 1976*.

Müllenhoff, Karl and Wilhelm Scherer. *Denkmäler Deutscher Poesie und Prosa aus dem VIII–XII Jahrhundert*, 5th ed. by Elias von Steinmeyer. Berlin: Weidmann, 1892.

Schlosser, Horst Dieter. *Althochdeutsche Literatur*. Frankfurt/M.: Fischer, 1970, rev. ed. 1989*.

Schlosser, Horst Dieter. *Althochdeutsche Literatur. Eine Textauswahl mit Übertragungen*. Berlin: Schmidt, 1998*.

Steinmeyer, Elias von. *Die kleineren althochdeutschen Sprachdenkmäler*. Berlin: Weidmann, 1916, repr. 1963.

Tschirch, Fritz. *Frühmittelalterliches Deutsch*. Halle/S.: Niemeyer, 1955.

Wipf, Karl A. *Althochdeutsche poetische Texte*. Stuttgart: Reclam, 1992*.

II. *Surveys, Collections, and Encyclopaedic Works*

Baesecke, Georg. *Kleinere Schriften zur althochdeutschen Sprache und Literatur*, ed. Werner Schröder. Berne and Munich: Francke, 1966.

Bergmann, Rolf, Heinrich Tiefenbach, and Lothar Voetz (edd.). *Althochdeutsch*. Heidelberg: Winter, 1987.

Bergmann, Rolf (ed.). *Althochdeutsche und altsächsische Literatur*. Berlin: de Gruyter, 2013 (articles from the *Verfasserlexikon* encyclopaedia; see Ruh, below).

Bertau, Karl. *Deutsche Literatur im europäischen Mittelalter. I. 800-1197*. Munich: Beck, 1972.

Bostock, J. Knight. *A Handbook on Old High German Literature*, 2nd ed. rev. K. C. King and D. R. McLintock. Oxford: Clarendon, 1976.

De Boor, Helmut. *Die deutsche Literatur von Karl dem Grossen bis zum Beginn der höfischen Dichtung* 770-1170. Munich: Beck, 1955.

Edwards, Cyril. *The Beginnings of German Literature: Comparative and Interdisciplinary Approaches to Old High German*. Rochester, NY: Camden House, 2002.

Ehrismann, Gustav. *Geschichte der deutschen Literatur bis zum Ausgang des Mittelalters. I. Die althochdeutsche Literatur*. Munich: Beck, 1954.

Flood, John L. and David N. Yeandle (edd.). *Mit regulu bithuungan: Neue Arbeiten zur althochdeutschen Poesie und Sprache*. Göppingen: Kümmerle, 1989.

Green, D. H. *Medieval Listening and Reading: The Primary Reception of German Literature 800-1300*. Cambridge: CUP, 1994.

Groseclose, John S. and Brian Murdoch. *Die althochdeutschen poetischen Denkmäler*. Stuttgart: Metzler, 1976.

Hammerich, Frederik. *Aelteste christliche Epik der Angelsachsen, Deutschen und Nordländer,* trans. (from Danish) A. Michelsen. Gütersloh: Bertelsmann, 1874.

Hasty, Will, and James Hardin. *Dictionary of Literary Biography: German Writers and Works of the Early Middle Ages.* New York: Gale, 1995.

Haubrichs, Wolfgang. *Die Anfänge: Versuche volkssprachiger Schriftlichkeit im frühen Mittelalter (ca. 700-1050/60).* Frankfurt/M.: Athenäum, 1988. (= *Geschichte der deutschen Literatur,* ed. Joachim Heinzle, I/i).

Kartschoke, Dieter. *Altdeutsche Bibeldichtung.* Stuttgart: Metzler, 1975.

Knapp, Fritz Peter. *Die Literatur des Früh- und Hochmittelalters.* Graz: Akademische Druck- und Verlagsanstalt, 1994 (Austrian literature).

Murdoch, Brian. *Old High German Literature.* Boston: Twayne, 1983.

Murdoch, Brian. "The Carolingian Period and the Early Middle Ages." In *Cambridge History of German Literature,* edited by H. Watanabe, 1–39. Cambridge: CUP, 1997.

Murdoch, Brian and Malcolm Read (edd.). *Early Germanic Literature and Culture.* (The Camden House History of German Literature I). Rochester: Camden House, 2004.

Murdoch, Brian (ed.). *German Literature of the Early Middle Ages.* (The Camden House History of German Literature II). Rochester: Camden House, 2004.

Ruh, Kurt et al. (edd). *Die deutsche Literatur des Mittelalters. Verfasserlexikon,* 2nd ed. Berlin and New York: de Gruyter, 1978–2008.

Rupp, Heinz. *Forschung zur althochdeutschen Literatur 1945–1962.* Stuttgart: Metzler, 1965.

Salmon, Paul. *Literature in Medieval Germany.* London: Cresset, 1967.

Schlosser, Horst Dieter. *Die literarischen Anfänge der deutschen Sprache.* Berlin: Schmidt, 1977.

Schneider, Hermann. *Heldendichtung, Geistlichendichtung, Ritterdichtung.* Heidelberg: Winter, 1943.

Schröder, Werner. *Grenzen und Möglichkeiten einer althochdeutschen Literaturgeschichte.* Leipzig: Sächsische Akademie, 1959.

Sonderegger, Stefan. *Althochdeutsch in St Gallen.* St Gallen: Ostschweiz, 1970.

Sonderegger, Stefan. *Althochdeutsche Sprache und Literatur.* Berlin: de Gruyter, 1974; 2nd ed. 2003.

Unwerth, Wolf von and Theodor Siebs. *Geschichte der deutschen Literatur bis zur Mitte des elften Jahrhunderts.* Berlin and Leipzig: de Gruyter, 1920.

Walshe, M. O'C. *Medieval German Literature.* London: Routledge and Kegan Paul, 1962.

III. *Other Works Cited in the Present Volume*

Abernethy, George William. *The Germanic Metrical Charms.* University of Wisconsin: Doctoral Dissertation, 1983.

Archibald, Linda. *Cur scriptor hunc librum theotisce dictaverit: The Educational Purpose of Otfrid's Evangelienbuch.* University of Stirling: Doctoral Dissertation, 1989.

Beck, Heinrich. *Das Ebersignum im Germanischen.* Berlin: de Gruyter, 1965.

Behaghel, Otto (ed.). *Heliand und Genesis,* 10th ed. by Burkhard Taeger. Tübingen: Niemeyer, 1996.

Belkin, Johanna and Jürgen Meier. *Bibliographie zu Otfrid von Weissenburg und zur altsächsischen Bibeldichtung.* Berlin: Schmidt, 1975.

Berg, Elisabeth. "Das *Ludwigslied* und die Schlacht bei Saucourt." *Rheinische Vierteljahrsblätter* 29 (1964): 175–199.

Bergmann, Rolf. "Zu der althochdeutschen Inschrift aus Köln." *Rheinische Vierteljahrsblätter* 30 (1965): 66–69 (with an illustration).

Cianci, Eleonora. *Incantesimi e benedizioni nella letteratura tedesca medievale (IX-XIII sec).* Göppingen: Kümmerle, 2004.

Dittrich, Marie Luise. "De Heinrico." *Zeitschrift für deutsches Altertum* 84 (1952/3): 274–308.

Edwards, Cyril and Jennie Kiff-Hooper. "Ego bonefacius scripsi? More Oblique Approaches to the Wessobrunn Prayer." In *Mit regulu bithuungan: Neue Arbeiten zur althochdeutschen Poesie und Sprache,* edited by John L. Flood and David N. Yeandle, 94–122. Göppingen: Kümmerle, 1989.

Edwards, Cyril. "*winileodos?* Zu Nonnen, Zensur und den Spuren des althochdeutschen Liebeslyrik." In *Theodisca,* edited by Wolfgang Haubrichs et al., 189–206. Berlin and New York: de Gruyter, 2000 (on *Hirsch und Hinde*).

Eis, Gerhard. *Altdeutsche Zaubersprüche.* Berlin: de Gruyter, 1964.

Elliott, Ralph W. V. "Byrhtnoth and Hildebrand: A Study in Heroic Technique." *Comparative Literature* 14 (1962): 53–70.

Ernst, Ulrich. *Der Liber Evangeliorum Otfrids von Weissenburg.* Cologne and Vienna: Böhlau, 1975.

Finger, Heinz. *Untersuchungen zum "Muspilli."* Göppingen: Kümmerle, 1977.

Fouracre, Paul. "The Context of the OHG 'Ludwigslied'." *Medium Aevum* 54 (1985): 87–103.

Fouracre, Paul. "Using the Background to the *Ludwigslied.* Some Methodological Problems." In *Mit regulu bithuungan. Neue Arbeiten zur althochdeutschen Poesie und Sprache,* edited by John L. Flood and David N. Yeandle, 80–93. Göppingen: Kümmerle, 1989.

Frings, Theodor. "Hirsch und Hinde." *Beiträge zur Geschichte der deutschen Sprache und Literatur*/Halle 85 (1963): 22–26.

Fuller, Susan. "Pagan Charms in Tenth-Century Saxony? The Function of the Merseburg Charms." *Monatshefte* 72 (1980): 162–170 (with a "Rejoinder" by Heather Stuart and F. Walla in *Germanic Notes* 14 (1983): 35–37).

Gamber, Klaus. "Das altbairische Petruslied." In *Sacerdos et cantus Gregoriani magister: Festschrift Ferdinand Haberl,* edited by Franz A. Stein, 107–116. Regensburg: Bosse, 1977.

Gutenbrunner, Siegfried. *Von Hildebrand und Hadubrand: Lied-Sage-Mythos*. Heidelberg: Winter, 1976.

Hagen, Sivert N. "Muspilli." *Modern Philology* 1 (1904): 397–409.

Hampp, Irmgard. "Vom Wesen des Zaubers im Zauberspruch." *Der Deutschunterricht* 13/1 (1961): 58–76.

Händl, Claudia. *Ludwigslied. Canto di Ludovico. Introduzione e commento*. Alessandria: Edizioni dell'Orso, 1990.

Hartmann, Reinildis. *Allegorisches Wörterbuch zu Otfrieds von Weissenburg Evangeliendichtung*. Munich: Fink, 1975.

Harvey, Ruth. "The Provenance of the Old High German *Ludwigslied*." *Medium Aevum* 14 (1945): 1–20.

Haubrichs, Wolfgang. *Ordo als Form*. Tübingen: Niemeyer, 1969.

Haubrichs, Wolfgang. *Georgslied und Georgslegende im frühen Mittelalter*. Königsstein/T.: Scriptor, 1979.

Hellgardt, Ernst. *Die exegetischen Quellen von Otfrids Evangelienbuch*. Tübingen: Niemeyer, 1981.

Helm, Karl. "Zur althochdeutschen 'Hausbesegnung'." *Beiträge zur Geschichte der deutschen Sprache und Literatur* 69 (1947): 358–361.

Henning, R. "Kleine Mitteilungen. *Starzfidere*." *Zeitschrift für deutsches Altertum* 30 (1908–1909): 111f.

Herweg, Mathias. *Ludwigslied, De Heinrico, Annolied*. Wiesbaden: Reichert, 2002.

Hoffmann von Fallersleben, A. H. *Geschichte des deutschen Kirchenliedes* [1861]. Hildesheim: Olms, 1965, 8–29.

Jongeboer, Henk. "Der Lorscher Bienensegen und der ags. Charm *wiþ ymbe*." *Amsterdamer Beiträge zur älteren Germanistik* 21 (1984): 63–70.

Jungandreas, Wolfgang. "De Heinrico." *Leuvense Bijdragen* 57 (1968): 75–91.

Kip, H. Z. "Ein unverstandener ahd. Spottvers." *MLN* 23 (1908): 106–108. (on the first satirical verse).

Kleiber, Wolfgang. *Otfrid von Weissenburg. Untersuchung zur handschriftlichen Überlieferung und Studien zum Aufbau des Evangelienbuches*. Berne and Munich: Francke, 1971.

Kleiber, Wolfgang. *Otfrid von Weissenburg*. Darmstadt: Wissenschaftliche Buchgesellschaft, 1978 (collection of essays).

Kolb, Herbert. "*Vora demo muspille*. Versuch einer Interpretation." *Zeitschrift für deutsches Altertum* 83 (1964): 2–33.

Kolbe, P. R. "Variation in the Old High German Post-Otfridian Poems." *MLN* 28 (1913): 216–217.

Kolbe, P. R. "The Strophic Form of the *Georgslied*." *MLN* 31 (1916): 19–23.

Krogmann, Willy. *Der althochdeutsche "138. Psalm": forschungsgeschichtlicher Überblick und Urfassung*. Hamburg: Wittig, 1973.

Lefrancq, Paul. *"Rhythmus Teutonicus" ou "Ludwigslied."* Paris: Droz, 1945.

Ludwig, Otto. "Der althochdeutsche und der biblische Psalm 138. Ein Vergleich." *Euphorion* 56 (1962): 402–409.

Lühr, Rosemarie. *Studien zur Sprache des Hildebrandsliedes*. Frankfurt am Main, Berne: Peter Lang, 1982.

Magoun, Francis P. "Otfrid's *Ad Liutbertum*." *PMLA* 58 (1943): 869–890.

Manganella, Gemma. "*Muspilli*. Problemi i interpretazioni." *Annali dell'Istituto Orientale di Napoli*/Sez. Germ. 3 (1960): 17–49.

Maurer, Friedrich. "Zur Frage nach der Heimat des Gedichtes Christus und die Samariterin." *Zeitschrift für deutsche Philologie* 54 (1929): 175–179.

Maurer, Friedrich. "Hildebrandslied und Ludwigslied." *Der Deutschunterricht* 9/2 (1957): 5–15.

McDonald, William C. "'Too Softly a Gift of Treasure': A Rereading of the Old High German *Hildebrandslied*." *Euphorion* 78 (1984): 1–16.

McKenzie, Donald A. *Otfrid von Weissenburg: Narrator or Commentator?* Stanford: Stanford University Press, 1946.

Menhardt, Hermann. "Die Überlieferung des althochdeutschen 138. Psalms." *Zeitschrift für deutsches Altertum* 77 (1940): 76–84.

Miller, Carol Ann. *The Old High German and Old Saxon Charms.* Washington University: Doctoral Dissertation, 1963.

Minis, Cola. *Handschrift, Form und Sprache des Muspilli.* Berlin: Schmidt, 1966. (Reviewed by Leslie Seiffert. *Modern Language Review* 64 (1969): 206–208).

Mohr, Wolfgang and Walter Haug. *Zweimal "Muspilli."* Tübingen: Niemeyer, 1977. (Reviewed by Brian Murdoch. *Medium Aevum* 47 (1978): 340–342).

Müller-Blattau, Joseph. "Zu Form und Überlieferung der ältesten deutschen geistlichen Lieder." *Zeitschrift für Musikwissenschaft* 17 (1935): 129–148.

Murdoch, Brian. "Saucourt and the *Ludwigslied.*" *Revue belge d'histoire et de philologie* 55 (1977): 841–867.

Murdoch, Brian. *The Germanic Hero: Politics and Pragmatism in Early Medieval Poetry.* London: Hambledon, 1996, 34–46.

Murdoch, Brian. "But Did They Work? Interpreting the Old High German Merseburg Charms in their Medieval Context." *Neuphilologische Mitteilungen* 89 (1988): 358–369.

Murdoch, Brian. "*Drohtin, uuerthe so!* Zur Funktionsweise der althochdeutschen Zaubersprüche." *Jahrbuch der Görres-Gesellschaft* NS 32 (1991): 11–37.

Naumann, Hans. "Der große Eber." *Beiträge zur Geschichte der deutschen Sprache und Literatur* 45 (1921): 473–477.

Norman, Frederick. *Three Essays on the Hildebrandslied.* London: Institute of Germanic Studies, 1973.

Ochs, Ernst. "*Ambo vos aequivoci.* Zur Abfassungszeit des ahd-lat. Heinrichslied." *Zeitschrift für deutsche Philologie* 66 (1941): 10–12.

Pakis, Valentine A. "The Literary Status of *Muspilli* in the History of Scholarship." *Amsterdamer Beiträge zur älteren Germanistik* 65 (2009): 41–60.

Pakis, Valentine A. "Sharing vessels with an *Armez Wib*: Jesus and the Samaritan Woman in Medieval Germanic." *Journal of English and Germanic Philology* 104 (2006): 514–527.

Pakis, Valentine A. "Line One of 'Christus und die Samariterin' (ÖNB 515)." *Zeitschrift für deutsche Philologie* 129 (2010): 441–448.

Patzlaff, Rainer. *Otfrid von Weissenburg und die mittelalterliche versus-Tradition.* Tübingen: Niemeyer, 1975.

Pezzo, Rafaella del. "Cristo e la Samaritana." *Annali dell'Istituto Orientale di Napoli/Sez. Germ.* 14 (1971): 105–116.

Renoir, Alain. "The Armor of the *Hildebrandslied.* An Oral-Formulaic Point of View." *Neuphilologische Mitteilungen* 78 (1977): 389–95.

Schädel, B. "Der heber gat in litun." *Zeitschrift für deutsche Philologie* 9 (1878): 93–99.

Schützeichel, Rudolf. *Codex Pal. Lat. 52.* Göttingen: Vandenhoek und Ruprecht: 1982.

Schwab, Ute. "Eber, aper und porcus in Notkers des Deutschen 'Rhetorik'", *Annali dell'Istituto Orientale di Napoli/Sez. Ling.* 8 (1967): 1–137.

Schwab, Ute. "Das althochdeutsche Lied 'Hirsch und Hinde' in seiner lateinischen Umgebung." In *Latein und Volkssprache im deutschen Mittelalter 1100-1500*, edited by Nikolaus Henkel and Nigel F. Palmer, 74–122. Tübingen: Niemeyer, 1992.

Schwab, Ute and Maria Vittoria Molinari. *Ildebrando: Quattro saggi e i testi.* Alessandria: Edizioni dell'Orso, 2001. (essays in English, Italian and German, including one of those by Norman, above).

Schwab, Ute. "'Hirez runeta' und die lateinischen Randeinträge im Cod. Brux. 8860-8867. 'Hirsch und Hinde und die Otmar Antiphonen'" (1993). In *Weniger wäre. Ausgewählte kleine Schriften*, edited by Ute Schwab, 413–467. Vienna: Fassbaender, 2003.

Schwab, Ute. "Zum 'Wessobrunner Gebet': Eine Vorstellung und neue Lesungen" [1988/9]. In *Weniger wäre: Ausgewählte kleine Schriften*, edited by Astrid van Nahl and Onga Middel, 349–384. Vienna: Fassbaender, 2003.

Schwarz, Werner. "The 'Ludwigslied', a Ninth Century Poem." *Modern Language Review* 42 (1947): 467–473.

Seiffert, Leslie. "The Metrical Form and Composition of the *Wessobrunner Gebet*." *Medium Aevum* 31 (1962): 1–13.

Sievers, Eduard (ed.). *Heliand*. Halle/S.: Waisenhaus, 1878.

Spechtler, Franz Viktor. "Altes und neues Recht. Bemerkungen über neue Forschungen zum althochdeutschen 'Muspilli'." *Amsterdamer Beiträge zur älteren Germanistik* 15 (1980): 39–52.

Stavenhagen, Lee. "Das 'Petruslied'." *Wirkendes Wort* 17 (1967): 21–28.

Swinburne, Hilda. "Numbers in Otfrid's 'Evangelienbuch'." *Modern Language Review* 52 (1957): 195–202.

Tschirch, Fritz. "Der heilige Georg als *figura Christi*." In *Festschrift Helmut de Boor*. Tübingen: Niemeyer, 1966, 1–19.

Uhlirz, Mathilde. "Der Modus 'De Heinrico' und sein geschichtlicher Inhalt." *Deutsche Vierteljahresschrift* 26 (1952): 153–161.

Urmoneit, Erika. *Der Wortschatz des Ludwigsliedes im Umkreis der althochdeutschen Literatur*. Munich: Fink, 1973.

Venosa, Elena di. *Muspilli. Introduzione, Traduzione e Commento*. Pisa: Pisa University Press, 2023.

Vollmann-Profe, Gisela. *Kommentar zu Otfrids Evangelienbuch: Teil I: Widmungen, Buch I, i–xi*. Bonn: Habelt, 1976.

Willems, Fritz. "Der parataktische Satzstil im *Ludwigslied*," *Zeitschrift für deutsches Altertum* 85 (1954/5): 18–35.

Willems, Fritz. "Psalm 138 und althochdeutscher Stil." *Deutsche Vierteljahresschrift* 29 (1955): 429–446.

Yeandle, David. "The *Ludwigslied*: King, Church, and Context." In *Mit regulu bithuungan. Neue Arbeiten zur althochdeutschen Poesie und Sprache,* edited by John L. Flood and David N. Yeandle, 18–79. Göppingen: Kümmerle, 1989.